PENGUIN ⓟ CLASSICS

THE PENGUIN FREUD GENERAL EDITOR:
ADAM PHILLIPS

THE SCHREBER CASE

SIGMUND FREUD was born in 1856 in Moravia; between the ages
of four and eighty-two his home was Vienna: in 1938 Hitler's inva-
sion of Austria forced him to seek asylum in London, where he died
in the following year. His career began with several years of brilliant
work on the anatomy and physiology of the nervous system. He was
almost thirty when, after a period of study under Charcot in Paris,
his interests first turned to psychology; and after ten years of clinical work in Vienna (at first in collaboration with Breuer, an older colleague) he invented what was to become psychoanalysis. This began
simply as a method of treating neurotic patients through talking, but
it quickly grew into an accumulation of knowledge about the workings of the mind in general. Freud was thus able to demonstrate the
development of the sexual instinct in childhood and largely on the
basis of an examination of dreams, arrived at this fundamental discovery of the unconscious forces that influence our everyday thoughts
and actions. Freud's life was uneventful, but his ideas have shaped
not only many specialist disciplines, but also the whole intellectual
climate of the twentieth century.

ANDREW WEBBER is Senior Lecturer in the department of German
and at Cambridge University and a Fellow of Churchill College. He
has published widely on German literature of the nineteenth and
twentieth centuries, on film and on psychoanalysis. He is the author
of *The Doppelgänger: Double Visions in German Literature* (1996).

COLIN MACCABE teaches literature and film at the universities of
Exeter and Pittsburgh. His most recent books are *Performance* and
The Eloquence of the Vulgar.

ADAM PHILLIPS was formerly Principal Child Psychotherapist at
Charing Cross Hospital in London. He is the author of several books
on psychoanalysis including *On Kissing, Tickling and Being Bored,
Darwin's Worms, Promises, Promises* and *Houdini's Box.*

SIGMUND FREUD

The Schreber Case

Translated by ANDREW WEBBER
with an Introduction by COLIN MACCABE

PENGUIN BOOKS

PENGUIN BOOKS

Published by the Penguin Group
Penguin Group (USA) Inc., 375 Hudson Street, New York, New York 10014, U.S.A.
Penguin Books Ltd, 80 Strand, London WC2R 0RL, England
Penguin Books Australia Ltd, 250 Camberwell Road, Camberwell, Victoria 3124, Australia
Penguin Books Canada Ltd, 10 Alcorn Avenue, Toronto, Ontario, Canada M4V 3B2
Penguin Books India (P) Ltd, 11 Community Centre, Panchsheel Park, New Delhi – 110 017, India
Penguin Books (N.Z.) Ltd, Cnr Rosedale and Airborne Roads, Albany, Auckland, New Zealand
Penguin Books (South Africa) (Pty) Ltd, 24 Sturdee Avenue, Rosebank, Johannesburg 2196, South Africa

Penguin Books Ltd, Registered Offices:
80 Strand, London WC2R 0RL, England

*Psychoanalytische Bemerkungen über einen autobiographisch beschrieben Fall von Paranoia
(Dementia Paranoides) first published 1911 in Jahrbuch für psychoanalytische und
psychopathologische Forschungen 3 (1)*
English translation published in Penguin Books (U.K.) 2002
This edition published 2003

Sigmund Freud's German text collected in *Gesammelte Werke (1940–52)*
copyright © Imago Publishing Co., Ltd, London, 1943
Translation and editorial matter copyright © Andrew Webber, 2002
Introduction copyright © Colin MacCabe, 2002
All rights reserved

LIBRARY OF CONGRESS CATALOGING IN PUBLICATION DATA
Freud, Sigmund, 1856–1939.
[Psychoanalytische Bemerkungen über einen autographisch
beschriebenen Fall von Paranoia (Dementia paranoides). English.]
The Schreber case / Sigmund Freud ; translated by Andrew Webber,
with an introduction by Colin MacCabe.
p. cm.
Includes selections from D. P. Schreber's Denkwürdigkeiten eines Nervenkranken.
ISBN 0 14 24.3742 5
1. Schreber, Daniel Paul, 1842–1911—Mental health.   2. Paranoia—Case studies.
I. Schreber, Daniel Paul, 1842–1911. Denkwürdigkeiten eines Nervenkranken. Selections.
2003. II. Title
RC520.F7313 2003
616.89'7—dc21   2003043319

Set in Adobe New Caledonia

Contents

Introduction

In 1903 the Leipzig publishing house Oswald Mutze brought out a volume entitled *Denkwürdigkeiten eines Nervenkranken* [*Memoirs of a Nervous Illness*] by the judge Daniel Paul Schreber. In his Preface the eminent Saxon lawyer explains his reasons for publication as follows:

I shall try to given an at least partly comprehensible exposition of supernatural matters, knowledge of which has been revealed to me for almost six years. I cannot of course count upon being fully understood because things are dealt with which cannot be expressed in human language; they exceed human understanding. Nor can I maintain that everything is irrefutably certain even for me: much remains only presumption and probability. After all I too am only a human being and therefore limited by the confines of human understanding; but one thing I am certain of, namely that I have come infinitely closer to the truth than human beings who have not received divine revelation.[1]

Schreber's book describes the history of his mental illness, from the inside of that illness. He is well aware of how his behaviour has been understood and categorized by psychiatrists, indeed Schreber includes a number of fascinating appendices which give full details of the medical and legal opinions in this case. Shortly after being appointed to the prestigious position of Senatspräsident in 1893 Schreber, for the second time in his life, found himself in a mental hospital. The first occasion, which followed his defeat in the 1884 elections for the German parliament, was diagnosed as hypochondria and did not involve hallucinations or paranoid fantasies. This second illness was very different. In February 1894, after more than two months in the same asylum and with the same Dr Flechsig who had previously cured him successfully, Schreber went through a night that brought on a total mental collapse. His body racked by spontaneous orgasms (the pedantic lawyer specifies half a dozen), his mind disintegrated. Through the complicated story that he then tells two features stand out. One, Schreber is convinced that he is to be transformed into a woman; two, he is being persecuted. Schreber himself is very clear of the centrality of sexual identity to his case. Reflecting on the period before his illness he notes that he had dreams that his first illness had recurred and: 'Furthermore, one morning while still in bed (whether still half asleep or already awake I cannot remember), I had a feeling which, thinking about it later when fully awake, struck me as highly peculiar. It was the idea that it really must be rather pleasant to be a woman succumbing to intercourse.'[2]

In the first instance, Schreber's paranoia focuses on Flechsig and the *Memoirs* suggest clearly that the motive for Flechsig's persecution of Schreber is sexual. After a prolonged period of crisis, however, the persecuting force that wishes to transform Schreber into a woman is identified as God. Furthermore, God's desire to impregnate Schreber and save the world is located in the future and thus Schreber is able to achieve an extraordinary balance. His former personality is reconstituted entirely and this is evident in the style and form of the *Memoirs* as well as in the evidence provided by his doctor in the legal appendix. At the same time, as the content of the *Memoirs* makes plain, he has an extraordinarily developed fantasy, which covers both his past persecution by both God and Flechsig and his future transformation into a woman and God's bride. While there remain symptoms in his everyday behaviour – he is an occasional transvestite and is also subject to fits of wordless bellowing – for the most part Schreber balances a totally sane and a totally insane self in a rare psychic settlement. It is this settlement that allows the life of a model citizen to coexist with a completely insane world of upper and lower Gods, of voluptuous nerves and of every daily occurrence necessitating a direct divine intervention.

From the first Schreber's readership was most significantly

composed of professional psychiatrists. The publishing house that allowed Schreber's work to find a public was what would nowadays be called a New Age institution, mixing mysticism and medicine. But there do not seem to have been any readers who were tempted to classify Schreber with the great mystics such as Meister Eckhart and Theresa of Lisieux. Schreber's account of his encounters with God bear no relation to texts of genuine religious experience above all because there is no sense of Schreber being involved and transformed by the experiences he undergoes. Indeed it is important to recognize that the text is written in a totally objective discourse – a mixture of law and medicine. One of the striking features of Schreber's text is how close it is to Freud; the weighing up of evidence and opinion, the examination of the possible explanations and then the determination to stick to his conclusions, even if he finds himself in a minority of one, make patient and doctor inhabitants of the same discursive universe. At the same time Freud's text (published as *Psychoanalytic Remarks on an Autobiographically Described Case of Paranoia (Dementia Paranoides)*), objective as it is, always bears witness to a mind transformed by the experiences he relates and the concepts he articulates; Schreber is at the end as he was at the beginning, the self-righteous judge: his constructed subjectivity untouched by the marvels he recounts.

But Schreber immediately found an audience among psychiatrists. One early reviewer recommended the book to all psychiatrists: 'Never before have the symptoms of paranoia been offered in such detail and so completely . . . because of his high intelligence and logical training, Schreber's presentation must be called perfect by the well-informed physician.'[3] This concern with symptoms and their description is of course constitutive of modern psychiatry. The great Kraeplin had not only divided the neuroses from the psychoses but had also split the psychosis into two: dementia praecox and manic depression. Bleuler in 1908 was to substitute the term schizophrenia for dementia praecox, and we currently seem to be living through a renaming of manic depression as bi-polar affective disorder, but the fundamental clinical picture of psychoses was then as it is now.

In fact this clinical picture is nowhere near as clear-cut as the textbooks might suggest but the more fundamental distinction between neurosis and psychosis is easier to grasp. The neurotic is he or she who is troubled by fantasies, by obsessional routines that avert some unspecified disaster, by hysterical fears of sexuality that have no basis in reality. The neurotic is, however, unhappy about his or her behaviour and wishes to alter it – of course he or she does not really wish to alter it, the neurotic symptom that combines both repression and the return of the repressed is too precious to be given up, but the neurotic is unhappy about its existence and aware that it poses a real problem. The psychotic is not troubled by fantasy but by reality – by the voices that speak to her, by the hallucinations that beset him. But the psychotic does not regard the ontological status of these hallucinations as problematic. While the neurotic knows that his fantasies set him apart from the world and in need of help, the psychotic finds in reality the absolute assurance of the centrality of his existence. Or, to put it another way, the neurotic wants to be cured, the psychotic does not. Yet again: and this time in psychoanalytic terms, the neurotic comes to the analyst desperate to set up that transferential relationship with the analyst which will enable his deepest identifications and meanings to be reworked while the psychotic has no investment in establishing or sustaining any relationship with anyone.

Astonishingly, although Freud was already by 1911 one of the most famous names in psychology and psychiatry he had never, except incidentally, treated psychotic patients. It was for financial reasons and because of his desire to marry that Freud had abandoned his promising career as a research scientist to become a general practitioner specializing in nervous diseases. His consulting rooms, full of the hysterical and obsessional neuroses of the Viennese middle class, provided the laboratory where psychoanalysis was discovered and where the talking cure was elaborated. But the discovery and the elaboration took place with neurotics. Any psychotic patient that presented him or herself in Freud's consulting rooms would, by the very nature of their condition, swiftly either refuse treatment or be referred on to a hospital. So even though Bleuler had acknowledged the importance of the Freudian conception of the psyche in the elaboration of the new configuration of psychosis around schizophrenia, Freud had never really addressed the question of psychosis. Indeed Freud reminds us at the beginning of his own reading that he has little clinical experience of psychosis. Given these facts it is a minor mystery that Freud did not read the text until seven years after it had been published although he clearly knew that it had already been much discussed in psychiatric circles. One might speculate that Freud's late reading of this text may find an explanation in its publishing provenance. Freud was a determined rationalist who was constantly concerned lest his life's discovery of the unconscious would slip into irrationalism. And indeed it is probably crucial to understand Freud's Schreber Case as an attempt to defend the centrality of sexuality to psychoanalytic theory. Towards the end of his life Jung was to recall a conversation with Freud from 1910:

I still remember vividly that Freud said to me: 'My dear Jung promise me you will never abandon the theory of sexuality. That is the most essential thing. You see we must make a dogma of it, an unshakeable bulwark' . . . Somewhat astonished, I asked him: 'A bulwark – against what?' Whereupon he answered, 'Against the black muddy tide,' here he hesitated for a moment, and then added 'of occultism.'[4]

Freud's Schreber text is explicitly dismissive of Adler's attempts to locate the workings of the psyche in social relations but, by the time Freud started work on Schreber, a total break with Adler was already inevitable. On the other hand Jung, who is quoted very favourably in the text, must be completely won over to the specific sexual constitution of the unconscious rather than lapsing into some generalized account of hidden forces within the mind. Through the 1890s, working with patients and on his own psychic life, Freud developed a new theory of the mind in which our conscious selves are merely one aspect of a more general process by which an individual animal body becomes a human being. Another aspect of this process is the necessary production of an unconscious, an unconscious that manifests itself in slips and dreams as well as more dramatically in neurotic symptoms. But Freud was absolutely convinced that the key term in the constitution of the unconscious and its relations to the conscious mind was sexuality and specifically the incest taboo. It is crucial to recognize that for Freud these two concepts are fundamentally interdependent, but it is also crucial to realize that Freud himself never fully demonstrated their necessary articulation. That the unconscious existed was clear from the moment in Charcot's lecture theatre that the great French master of psychiatry produced examples of hysterical paralysis in which patients would have genuinely paralysed limbs but the limbs thus paralysed did not correspond to anatomical reality (the muscles of the leg stretch up in to the lower back) but to linguistic representation (the paralysed leg was the leg of non-scientific language). And psychoanalysis with its method of free association, slips, dreams and its consequent concepts of resistance and transference developed the reality of this unconscious over the next twenty years. But there are, as it were, two constant dangers of misinterpretation of the unconscious. On the one hand there will be desires to ground it in a more specific social reality, what one might in an archaic political language call 'a left deviation', on the other to place it in relation to a more universal mythology grounded in biology, a corresponding 'right deviation'.

When Freud sat down to write the Schreber Case these alternatives were not just imaginary possibilities; they were two real theoretical and institutional threats to the new science of psychoanalysis. From very early in the 1900s Freud had gathered around him in Vienna a group with whom he would discuss and develop psychoanalysis. All Jews and most general practitioners like himself, there is no doubt that the most brilliant and charismatic of this group was Alfred Adler, a committed member of the Social Democratic Party and a doctor whose patients were from much poorer classes than Freud's. Freud's books and the theories of psychoanalysis were also, however, finding audiences all over the world. The most important of these initial audiences was to be found in Zurich at the world-famous Burgholzli Mental Hospital. And the most important of these readers was Carl Gustav Jung, the son of a pastor and much concerned with questions of religion.

Freud seized on his new Zurich adherents, and particularly Jung, with enthusiasm. Jung bought much more scientific and psychiatric credibility than the admittedly oddball crew that had gathered round Freud in Vienna and, crucially, he was not a Jew. Freud was obsessed with the fear that psychoanalysis would be dismissed as a 'Jewish science'; Jung was the guarantee it would make it out of the ghetto. And it was Jung, who as a hospital psychiatrist had much more experience of psychoses, who urged Freud to read Schreber.

This was a reading whose power and afterlife might have surprised even the megalomaniac Schreber. A first trawl through the MLA bibliography reveals more than 150 articles and books on the demented German jurist and the last decade has seen a veritable explosion of glosses and commentaries. Much of this debate turns on Freud's interpretation of Schreber's madness as underpinned by repressed homosexuality. For Freud the paranoid Schreber is assailed by the unacceptable thought 'I love Flechsig', which becomes transformed into the acceptable thought 'Flechsig hates me'. While there can be no doubt of the brilliance of Freud's interpretative schemas, there can also be no doubt that this interpretation is much less compelling than his synopsis of the case. The problem is that there is no account of why Schreber's unconscious homosexual wish could not either have passed into consciousness in explicitly homosexual form or have been sublimated in the way that Freud celebrates in his own case. Writing to Ferenczi about his own psychic constitution a couple of years earlier, and around the time of his first elaboration of a relation between paranoia and repressed homosexuality, he says, 'A piece of homosexual investment has been withdrawn and utilized for the enlargement of my own ego. I have succeeded where the paranoiac fails'.[5] But this talk of success and failure is deeply misleading in so far as it suggests, completely contrary to Freud's theory, that it is a conscious decision to choose between repression and sublimation. What we need in order to understand the Schreber Case is a structure that would enable us to understand the relation between Schreber's sexual constitution and his descent into lunacy. For what Freud's theory promises us, a promise which he was, even as he wrote the Schreber Case, defending against Adler and Jung, is that the content of our unconscious lives is fundamentally structured by the recognition of sexual difference. Of Freud's heirs it was the French psychoanalyst Jacques Lacan who most ferociously defended the Freudian inheritance, and the recent increased interest in Schreber is in large measure due to the centrality of Schreber to Lacan's thinking.

Lacan's crucial emphasis is that Freud's teaching demonstrates that our objective external world and our inter-subjective relationships are functions of each other. To understand this we have to place language at the centre of our mental development in a way that Freud constantly suggests but never clearly articulates. Let us imagine the small infant assailed by numerous sensations. Of these perhaps the most insistent is hunger and the pain that it provokes. This pain unleashes the cry that at this moment is nothing but a biological signal to the mother. But the cry brings the mother and the breast that assuages the child's hunger. The child's gradual recognition that the cry is a sign which can be interpreted is at one and the same time the recognition of the mother as another person and of the breast as an object. With the advent of the sign we pass from the world of need (the cry is a signal of hunger) to the world of demand (the cry is addressed to the mother and can be produced independently of need). From the undifferentiated world of sensation, language summons forth the object and the other. But the presence of the object implies also its absence and the child is now inevitably introduced to the world of desire in which, even when need has been assuaged and demand has been answered, there is now a perpetual chain of presence and absence which constitutes desire. In order to grasp the functioning of this chain, and above all to avoid the risk of hallucination that it involves because the functioning of language allows for the potential presence of any object, the child has to accept that this chain exists independently of its own existence. It is here that the father intervenes in a relation with the mother from which the child is excluded but in which it is represented. In giving up its omnipotence, in realizing that the language in which he speaks to the mother is not his property, the child experiences that castration which marks his access to the human world in which it is a law of the enjoyment of any object that the mother has been renounced.[6] It is crucial to recognize, above all in the context of Schreber, that this intervention of the father is not to be understood in terms of the father as omnipotent cause of his own desire. That indeed is the first fantasy of the child because then castration can be avoided by acceding to the position of the father. The real moment of the Oedipus arrives, and with it that visceral hatred of the father which psychoanalysis finds so fundamental, at the moment the child realizes that the father is himself subject to the law.

Paradoxically, one could say that Schreber never achieved that hatred of his father, for his father offered an image of omnipotence which allowed the child to imagine that he could avoid castration, that he could speak a language entirely under his control. Freud describes Schreber's father in the following terms:

> The father of Justice Dr Schreber was in fact a man not without conse-quence. He was Dr Daniel Gottlob Moritz Schreber, whose memory is still preserved by the Schreber Associations, especially numerous in Saxony, a physician, no less, whose efforts to ensure the harmonious education of the young, the co-operation in this of family- and school-life, and the application of the care of the body and physical work to raising standards of health, were of lasting influence on his contemporaries. The many editions of his *Ärztliche Zimmergymnastik* [*Medical Home Gymnastics*] to be found among our circles bear witness to his reputation as the founder of therapeutic gymnastics in Germany. Such a father was certainly not unpredisposed to be transfigured into a God in the tender memory of his son who was robbed of him so early by death. (p. 40)

The *Medical Home Gymnastics* makes clear that Schreber *père* was the personal trainer from hell. There seems no ailment that cannot be cured by his ludicrous physical jerks. Indeed physical health becomes a crushing moral duty. Many of his son's fantasies, particularly his conviction at the most intense stage of his illness that his body is being systematically destroyed and reconstituted, would seem to lead clearly back to his father's exercises.[7] Freud himself makes clear how crucial the father is in Schreber's construction of

his God, both adored and mocked, feared and reviled. But Freud stops
short in his analysis, never seeming to ask himself the significance of
the almost total absence of mothers from the text. It is as if, at the
very moment when Freud is becoming 'the father of psychoanalysis',
he is unwilling to analyse the way in which a father can never be
anything more than a name and is thus unable to articulate Schreber's problem that his father never moves from an imaginary to a
symbolic register. But it is Lacan who develops the analysis so that
it is the father's omnipotence which is at one and the same time the
cause of Schreber's inability to symbolize his own femininity, and
this failure is the very cause of his hallucination and delirium. Where
Freud premises a homosexual desire, for which there is no structural
reason why it is unbearable, and an overweening father, Lacan posits
a failure in symbolization which produces both the psychic content
of the desire to be a woman and the structure of the psychosis.

For Lacan there is no possibility of understanding psychosis without recourse to the categories of the imaginary, the symbolic and
the real. The imaginary, a category developed within French
phenomenology and particularly by Jean-Paul Sartre and Maurice
Merleau Ponty, is the world of consciousness, of the ego. The
symbolic, a category which Lacan borrowed from Claude Levi-
Strauss and French anthropology, is the word of the social in so far
as that world is constituted by the possibility of symbolization: of one
thing standing for another. Ferdinand de Saussure's theory of language neatly maps on to this. The world of meaning, the world of
consciousness, the world of objects is the world of the signified. The
world of the matter of sound and writing, the formal articulation of
the language, is the world of the signifier. For Lacan this theory
enables one to understand how the world of consciousness and its
secure divisions – I am at the centre of my world which is at it is –
is constantly being undermined by the fact that this world only
appears within a specific language whose articulations have both
preceded and will survive my being in the world. More precisely the
structure of the signified and the signifier enable us to understand
Freud's teaching on the unconscious and repression. As I speak the
signifying chains of the language multiply infinitely, but in order to

make meaning, to be conscious, those chains must be ignored, or rather repressed because ignored might suggest a conscious choice whereas repressed tells us that this unconscious is a necessary feature of the control of speech. Lacan then goes further by linking this feature of language to sexuality. While Lévi-Strauss might be happy with an unconscious generally structured around exchange, Lacan, fierce Freudian that he is, insists that it is sexual difference symbolized by the phallus which is the key to successful speech. It is the recognition that we could be different, that we could be castrated, that we identify with both bottom and top in the primal scene, that we are fundamentally bisexual symbolically which enables us to assume an imaginary sexual identity. And this recognition is structured by language. It is here that Lacan becomes most difficult to follow for his vocabulary from Saussure of signifier and signified focuses on the language as indicative while it is clear that what is at stake here is the vocative: the address to another in interrogative or imperative mode.[8] The neurotic is a person who wishes at all costs to deny the unconscious, to hold signifier and signified rigidly together, to deny their bisexual constitution, but at the deepest level they have already accepted a symbolic castration and thus their problems come forth in hysterical or obsessional symptoms which can be deciphered in terms of the signifying chain that they are trying to deny. They are already willing to enter into a transferential relation because speech for them is fundamentally social. The psychotic has refused a symbolic castration with a mechanism which is not that of repression but of foreclosure (Lacan teases the term of *Verwerfung* out of Freud's texts). The psychotic has never accepted the real sociality of language, that which makes of his existence a mere link in the chain, because the father instead of introducing him to lack has held out the promise of an all-powerful existence. If the mother has been taken away from him, subtracted by her desire for another, the father promises to be cause of his own desire. The psychotic then never really uses language. Schreber's text is strikingly free of metaphor, the fundamental trope where we find ourselves transformed in language, just as it is almost completely free of femininity. Just as psychosis has a fundamentally different structure, that of

Verwerfung (foreclosure) rather than *Verdrangung* (repression), so the rejected signifier reappears not as an hysterical symptom in the body or an obsession in behaviour but as hallucination. Lacan talks of what has been rejected in the symbolic returning in the real. The real for Lacan is not reality, which is to be found in the realm of the imaginary, but the record of the genuine encounters of our existence – the conversations in which we have been made and the objects that resulted. For the neurotic this real has been internalized – it is what gives real point to the dialectic between imaginary and symbolic. For the psychotic the real has not been internalized and when Schreber encounters a situation in which it becomes clear that he has never really received any speech addressed to him, that he has never accepted the passive position, then what has been rejected from the symbolic, the possibility of his being a woman, returns in the real: he is to be transformed into a woman. Lacan's reading of Schreber complements and builds on Freud and has the huge theoretical advantage of distinguishing between neurosis and psychosis. It suffers, as does all of Lacan's theorizing, that the crucial moment of Schreber's existence, the moment when at the levels of the imaginary, the symbolic and the real the primordial signifier is rejected, is necessarily opaque to us. Only within an analysis, and then in a form which is unrepresentable outside the transferential relationship, can one discover that moment at which one's being in the world, one's sexual identity and the fundamental metaphoricity of language are articulated together. The only model outside analysis that Lacan offers, and that towards the end of his life and with a kind of querulous astonishment that it exists, is James Joyce's *Finnegans Wake*.

In recent decades readings of Schreber have begun to stress the social implications of Schreber's text. Elias Canetti was to read it as the precursor of another paranoid spiritual autobiography published twenty years later: Adolf Hitler's *Mein Kampf*. More recently Eric Santner's *My Own Private Germany* reads Schreber's crisis of symbolic authority not as the individual fate of Schreber but as indicative of a general crisis within Germany of which Nazism is the most terrifying symptom. Santner's book succeeds in articulating much more of Schreber's texts that Freud or Lacan: demonstrating how questions of the struggle between Catholicism and Protestantism are centrally inscribed in the text and how the question of femininity necessarily involves the question of Judaism. There is, however, no conclusive argument as to why these problems produce a crisis of authority more pronounced in Germany that in other European countries. More worryingly there is an uncritical acceptance of Michel Foucault's so-called 'repressive hypothesis', which makes of psychoanalysis and its concern with the internalized representations of sexuality a mere symptom of a more general development of medical practices that 'produce' sexuality as the key term of identity. While Santner makes an excellent case for needing to locate Schreber and Freud's reading of him in a wider context, he makes no attempt to do this by developing the psychoanalytic account.

There are two levels at which this account needs to be developed. The first, and this is perhaps Santner's most brilliant contribution, is at the level of the institution of psychoanalysis itself. When Freud writes the Schreber Case history he is struggling to deal with the first splits in the psychoanalytic movement. There is no doubt that the parallels between Schreber's crisis on taking on his judgeship and Freud's problems as the father of psychoanalysis are striking. There is also no doubt that Freud's elaboration of the relation between paranoia and repressed homosexuality was developed from his relationship with his pupils and disciples. One is tempted to speculate that Freud assimilated Schreber's case too quickly to his own and thus failed to see the more fundamental symbolic quandary in which judge Schreber found himself. As we have argued, the text was written as part of an immediate and explicit attempt to counter Adler, who was in the process of splitting from the psychoanalytic movement, and as a less immediate and more implicit attempt to counter Jung, who would split from the psychoanalytic movement two years later. Indeed it was Freud's insistence on the sexual basis for psychosis as well as neurosis that crystallized for Jung his ineradicable differences with Freud. Adler's fundamental concept was that of 'the masculine protest'. Having its origins in a biological theory of organ inferiority, Adler's theory was in fact a version of that 'left deviation' (Foucault and Guattari would be contemporary parallels) in which the unconscious is simply the product of social forces. Leaving biology well behind Adler focused on the necessary feelings of inferiority incurred in any attempt to conform to impossible social claims. Schreber would seem custom made for an Adlerian analysis in which the impossibility of measuring up to the demands of his new job gave rise to a 'masculine protest', which produced the psychosis and its resolution in the fantasy of becoming a woman. Freud is determined to make clear that if there is a 'masculine protest' it rests on the side of the conscious and comes after the production of the feminine fantasy. He is determined to assert the primacy of the unconscious. If, however, we adopt a more symbolic reading in terms of the inability of Schreber to symbolize femininity this allows a reading which both stresses the reality of the unconscious but also allows a much more social understanding of that unconscious. For it is possible to ground the psychosis in the social ground of Schreber's father's notions of an obedient spirit in a healthy body in a pure German nation. Why Freud never follows the interpretation in this direction is difficult to explain but one might speculate that the figure of the father, and particularly Schreber *père*, a brilliant doctor who had started a social movement that bought medical concerns into daily life, was simply too close to home. At a time when he was unwilling to have his authority challenged, at a time when he was turning Jung into a psychotic son, further analysis of Schreber was too difficult.

Indeed the Schreber Case is above all addressed to Jung. Jung himself is fulsomely praised in the article, unlike Adler, who is dismissed in a contemptuous footnote, but Freud's aim is to make clear that Schreber's religious fantasies are not to be located in fundamental religious instincts but in sexual drives and their vicissitudes. If at one level of the text Freud arrests the analysis too easily at the level of repressed homosexual desire, at another he indicates a much more profound analysis with his first venture into anthropological theory. Much derided as the details have been, these anthropological theories are crucial to Freud if he is to find a resting place for the human between the pressures of the too-specific socializers and the too-universal mythologizers. In his anthropological theories

Freud is seeking an evolutionary account of the moment of the constitution of the unconscious. That he never managed to undertake the task does not in any way minimize its interest or importance.

Indeed if we look on psychoanalysis as seeking a new symbolic settlement, one in which the primacy of the unconscious is acknowledged and the symbolization of bisexuality emphasized, then it may be crucial to have a clearer picture of what one might term 'the history of the unconscious'. At this point the link between paranoia and repressed homosexuality may become much more historically specific than Freud would suggest. It may be that both Schreber and Freud should take their place in the context of a much more general 'coming out' from Wilde to Weininger which demonstrated across Europe at the turn of the century the inescapability of homosexual desire. There is no doubt that Freud saw the analysis of his own homosexuality as one of the key moments in the elaboration of psychoanalysis. But if one looks at the very sorry institutional history of psychoanalysis one might say that a possible reason for this history is Freud's failure to let that homosexuality feed into the institutional elaboration of psychoanalysis. The foreclosure of the interpretation of Schreber in relation to the father means that the crucial question of the relation to the mother and what would be involved in her adequate symbolization is never broached.

The second level at which the Schreber Case needs a social grounding is at the more general level not just of Germany but of Europe. Psychoanalysis does not by and large concern itself with social explanations but it is wrong to think that it does not have the concepts to do so. The Lacanian real is not limited to speech within the family – it includes all discourse where the subject has been addressed in his or her being. More pertinently to Schreber – it is in his paper 'On Narcissism', published three years after his Schreber Case and the indispensable companion piece to it, that Freud develops the notion of the ego ideal as one of the crucial elements in the outplaying of primary narcissism. In the concluding paragraph Freud writes: 'The ego ideal opens up an important avenue for the understanding of group psychology. In addition to its individual side, this ideal has a social side; it is also the common ideal of a family, a class or a nation' (*Standard Edition*, vol. XIV, p. 101). It is exactly the ego ideal, the crucial recognition of the third term that disrupts the binary relationship with the mother, of which Schreber knows nothing. The overpowerful father continues to offer an image with which Schreber's primary narcissism can identify. Indeed if behind Schreber's God we can discern the figure of the father then behind that is the even more terrifying figure of Schreber's Bauderlairean *semblable*. The endlessly dividing and aggressive God caught between the twin pole of attraction and aggression is none other than Schreber's own narcissistic self, impervious to the social world that has created it.

By a bizarre coincidence Freud published his analysis of Schreber in the same year as the judge died. After the death of his wife in 1907, Schreber suffered another collapse and was to spend his last four years in a new mental hospital outside Leipzig, consumed by ideas of his own decomposition and rotting.[9] Three years later Europe was to decompose and rot on the hideous battlefields of the First World War. The advent of a new century has made much clearer that the First World War is still the unfinished business of the West: that we are still struggling to find ego ideals genuinely able to free us from narcissistic aggression. The *memoirs* of Schreber and Freud's analysis of them are not merely historical curios; they still speak to our most abiding problems.

Colin MacCabe, 2001

Notes

1. Quoted from Daniel Paul Schreber, *Memoirs of My Nervous Illness*, tr. and ed. with Introduction, Notes and Discussion by Ida Macalpine and Richard A. Hunter (London: W. M. Dawson and Sons, 1955), p. 41.
2. Ibid., p. 66.
3. Ibid., p. 6.
4. Carl Gustav Jung, *Memories, Dream, Reflections* (London: Collins and Routledge Kegan Paul, 1964), pp. 147–8.
5. *The Correspondence of Sigmund Freud and Sandor Ferenczi* (Cambridge, MA: Harvard University Press, 1993), p. 43.

6. The paradox of castration is that it is the recognition of the impossibility of the desire for the mother that is the condition of the existence of desire at all. The moment that the imaginary penis becomes the symbolic phallus is the moment at which the child accepts that the existence of his own penis is not guaranteed by his mother's desire and that he must take his place in a social order in which desire is always a circulation involving a third term.

7. For more details of the Schreber Case history see W. G. Niederland, *The Schreber Case: Psychoanalytic Profile of a Paranoid Personality* (Hillsdale, NJ: Analytic Press 1984) and Zvi Lothan, *In Defense of Schreber: Soul Murder and Psychiatry* (Hillsdale, NJ: Analytic Press, 1992).

8. One of Lacan's great defects is his refusal at all points to put his questions within any form of research project which is not understood as grimly personal. Any real development of Lacan's theory will need to free it from this paranoid structure.

9. Eric L. Santner, *My Own Private Germany: Daniel Paul Schreber's Secret History of Modernity* (Princeton, NJ: Princeton University Press, 1996), p. 46.

Translator's Preface

The Schreber Case, published by Freud under the title *Psychoana-lytic Remarks on an Autobiographically Described Case of Paranoia (Dementia Paranoides)*, is distinctive in being based more or less entirely on the memoir of the conjectural patient. It thus has the status of a generic hybrid, somewhere between the case histories proper and the studies based on literary or other documentary material. In particular, Freud's analysis here accommodates considerable exposition through quotation from Schreber's own text and from the doctors' reports in the Schreber file. Switching between Freud's own voice and that of his analysand, the text therefore has an almost dialogic character. Freud famously suggested that his case histories read like novellas, and the Schreber Case can be said to correlate with a particular form of that genre, where a framework narrator discovers and then mediates a strange text written by another hand. Freud not only presents extended excerpts from Schreber's *Memoirs*, but also styles his analytic work on it as, in itself, a form of translation. In this he seeks, and claims, fidelity to the original, translating it into 'the technical terminology of medicine' without adding 'the slightest thing to its content'.

The task of the translator of this psychoanalytic 'novella' is to do justice, then, to two writers: Freud himself, as framing expositor and analytic translator; and the memoirist Schreber. Both have distinctive styles, and I have sought to render these as closely as possible, even where the style may be considered 'clumsy' because overladen or reiterative. Schreber's tendency to stretch syntax at his more exalted moments is in part mimicked by Freud; indeed, at points the two writers merge, as Freud cites Schreber in more indirect forms. Similarly, both have recourse to neologisms in order to communicate the more unconventional aspects of their respective systems, and both bring a range of cultural references to bear in the understanding of those systems. To echo Freud's description of Schreber's text, both can be said to incorporate 'borrowed and original elements'.

One of the most fascinating aspects of Freud's text is its tendency to adopt the terms of Schreber's own, especially when challenging the forces of censorship. The end of the introductory remarks sees Freud citing Schreber's words as a justification for publishing the case in spite of the possibility of offence to parties still living. Freud's text also imitates the omissions and 'singularities of style' demanded by censorship in the original, but argues that a text like Schreber's, and by extension his own, should be able to use terms like 'shit' and 'fuck' without compunction. Both writers allow the formal discourse of their reports to incorporate this colloquial language of bodily function. If the reports of Schreber's own physicians are on the whole tightly controlled by social and psychiatric protocol, Freud adopts a more identificatory voice in his handling of Schreber's language. The 'striking conformity' with his own theory, which Freud recognizes in Schreber's delusion, extends to a certain conformity of styling.

Aside from this citational relationship to Schreber's text (including the 'elementary language' that functions as a distinctive sub-discourse within it), Freud's narrative incorporates a variety of styles. It moves from the scientific to the personal, from the discursive conventions of Logic in the propositions of section III to the language of anthropology in the Postscript. It is exemplary of the extraordinary modality, the shifting of idiom, that characterizes Freud's writings in general and that places particular demands on the translator. The intention here has been to respect the details and the idiosyncrasies of these different styles of voice. An immediate example of this is given in the title where I have opted to retain Freud's somewhat ponderous styling with the formulation 'an autobiographically described case'. My aim throughout has been to resist the homogenization of such motley elements as well as to give the rhetorical verve that characterizes much of the writing its due.

While the Schreber essay presents fewer challenges in its technical vocabulary than many of Freud's texts, a glossary of some of the more debatable key terms, with an indication of the strategy behind their translation here, is given below.

angelehnt – attached   The adjective *angelehnt* is derived from the notion of the *Anlehnungstypus* of object-choice (what the *Standard Edition* calls the 'anaclitic' type). It suggests the two primary senses of *Anlehnung*: a choice of object at once based on emotional 'attachment' and forged 'by analogy with' pre-existing forms of relationship with others. I have chosen to emphasize the first of these two meanings.

Besetzung – investment   This term and its cognates might well have been translated using the 'cathexis' of the *Standard Edition*. No single term in English embraces the flexible resonances of the German original, including, in particular, the occupation of a position or a territory. I have opted, however, for 'investment' as a word that carries at least some of the connotations of *Besetzung*. While its economic sense introduces a different set of resonances, these are at least in keeping with the extensive repertory of economic metaphors that Freud adopts in order to figure the dynamic system of the drives as conduits of libidinal interest.

Durchbruch – breakthrough   The term is used here to describe the breaching of the work of repression.

Nachdrang – after-pressure   This neologism, used to describe the secondary element in the process of repression, needs to carry a sense of pressing, cognate with, but not identical to, repression at large.

Seelenleben – life of the soul   The term *Seele* is, I believe, something of an operative anachronism for Freud. Its metaphysical connotations are undoubtedly in tension with the materialistic tendency of his project, but that tension seems to me to be operative in the original and worth retaining. In particular, the term resonates the transcendental discourse of souls that characterizes Schreber's description of his delusion.

Triebe – drives   Most commentators find the 'instincts' of the

Standard Edition unsatisfactory. 'Drives' is now quite well established as an alternative and is certainly closer to the sense of impulsion that is fundamental to Freud's dynamic model.

Versagung – frustration   This describes the denial or non-fulfilment of a wish; a 'failure', that is, on the part of the world in relation to the subject's desires.

Andrew Webber, 2001

The Schreber Case

*Psychoanalytic Remarks on
an Autobiographically
Described Case of Paranoia
(Dementia Paranoides)*

[Introduction]

The analytic investigation of paranoia causes particular kinds of difficulty for physicians, like myself, not working in public institutions. We cannot accept patients suffering from this disorder, or at least cannot retain them for long, given that we set the prospect of therapeutic success as a precondition for our treatment. It is thus only exceptionally the case that I am able to gain a deeper insight into the structure of paranoia, whether because the uncertainty of a diagnosis (which is not always a simple matter) justifies the attempt at exerting some influence, or because I submit to the requests of the next of kin and agree to treat a patient of this kind for a time in spite of an assured diagnosis. Of course, I have many other opportunities to see those suffering from paranoia and dementia and I learn as much about them as other psychiatrists do about their cases, but this is not generally sufficient to reach analytic conclusions.

The psychoanalytic investigation of paranoia would not be possible at all if the patients were not peculiar in betraying, albeit in distorted form, precisely that which other neurotics hide away as a secret. As paranoiacs cannot be forced to overcome their inner resistances and in any case only say what they wish to say, precisely with respect to this disorder a written account or published case history may serve as a substitute for personal acquaintance with the patient. I am not therefore inclined to think it inadmissible to attach analytic interpretations to the case history of a paranoiac (one suffering from dementia paranoides) whom I have never seen, but who has described his own case history and, by going to print, put it into the public domain.

This is the case of the erstwhile Presiding Judge in the Saxon

Court of Appeal and doctor of law Daniel Paul Schreber, whose *Denkwürdigkeiten eines Nervenkranken* [*Memoirs of a Nervous Illness*] appeared in book form in 1903 and, to the best of my knowledge, provoked quite considerable interest among psychiatrists. It is possible that Dr Schreber is still alive today and has so retreated from the system of delusion represented in 1903 that these remarks on his book might cause him pain. In as far, however, as he still maintains the identity of his present personality with its earlier state, I can draw on arguments of his own, with which this 'intellectually superior man of unusually sharp mind and sharp powers of observation'[1] rebuffed attempts to keep him from going to print: 'In this I have not concealed from myself the concerns that seem to stand in the way of publication: in particular, consideration for several people still alive today. On the other hand, I am of the opinion that it may be of value to science and to the understanding of religious truths if, while I am still alive, qualified persons might be able to conduct certain observations of my body and my personal fate. This consideration must silence all personal ones.'[2] At another point in the book, he makes it known that he has decided to hold fast to the intention of publication, even if his doctor, Privy Councillor Dr Flechsig of Leipzig, should consider this to give grounds for a suit against him. He calls upon Flechsig in the same way that I now call upon him: 'I hope,' he writes, 'that on the part of Privy Councillor Prof. Flechsig, too, scientific interest in the contents of my Memoirs will overwhelm any personal sensitivities.'

While, in what follows, I am providing verbatim citations of all sections of the *Memoirs* that support my interpretations, I would ask readers of this study first to make themselves familiar with the book by reading it once at least.

Notes

1. This certainly not unjustified self-characterization is to be found on p. 35 of Schreber's book.
2. Preface to the *Memoirs*.

I

Case History

'I have twice suffered from nervous illness,' Dr Schreber reports, 'in either case as a result of intellectual over-exertion; on the first occasion (when I was presiding over the provincial court in Chemnitz) as a result of standing for the Reichstag, on the second as a result of the unusual burden of work that I encountered when I took up my new appointment as Presiding Judge of the Court of Appeal in Dresden' (p. 34).

The first illness emerged in the autumn of 1884 and was totally cured by the end of 1885. Flechsig, in whose clinic the patient spent six months at that time, described the condition, in a 'Pro forma Assessment' submitted later, as an attack of severe hypochondria. Dr Schreber attests that this illness ran its course 'without any occurrences bordering upon the transcendental domain' (p. 35).

Neither the patient's writings nor the appended assessments by his doctors provide sufficient information as to his earlier history and situation in life. I am not even able to say how old he was at the time he fell ill, though the high position he had reached in the judicial service before the second bout of illness would indicate a minimum age. We learn that at the time of his 'hypochondria' Dr Schreber had already long been married. He writes: 'The gratitude was perhaps still more heartfelt on the part of my wife, who revered Prof. Flechsig as the man who had no less than restored her husband to her, so that years later his picture was still standing on her desk' (p. 36). And further that 'After I recovered from my first illness I spent eight on the whole very happy years with my wife, years rich in public honours and only dimmed from time to time by the recurrent dashing of our hopes that the marriage might be blessed with children.'

In June 1893 he was given notice of his imminent appointment as Presiding Judge, and he took up office on 1 October of the same year. The interim period[1] is marked by several dreams, to which he was only later led to attach significance. He more than once dreamt that his earlier nervous illness had returned and was as unhappy about this during the dream as he was happy when he discovered upon waking that it had indeed been only a dream. Also, one early morning, in a state between sleep and waking, he had 'the notion that it must really be a rather nice thing to be a woman undergoing intercourse' (p. 36), an idea he would have found outrageous when fully conscious.

The second illness began with torturous insomnia at the end of October 1893, leading him to return to Flechsig's clinic, where his condition, however, rapidly deteriorated. An account of the illness's further development is given in a later Assessment filed by the director of the Sonnenstein Asylum (p. 380): 'At the start of his stay there[2] he expressed more hypochondriac ideas, complaining that he was suffering from softening of the brain and would soon die, etc., but notions of persecution were already mixed into the overall clinical picture, owing to the appearance of sensory delusions, albeit isolated at first, while at the same time acute hyperaesthesia, considerable sensitivity to light and noise, set in. Later the visual and auditory delusions became more frequent and, in association with coenaesthetic disturbances, governed all his feelings and thoughts; he held himself to be dead and rotting, suffering from the plague, imagined that all manner of dreadful manipulations were being carried out on his body, and, as he himself now puts it, went through things more terrible than have ever been imagined, and this for a holy purpose. The pathological ideation took such hold of the patient that, not amenable to any other impression, he sat rigidly for hours on end in an hallucinatory stupor, while, on the other hand, it tormented him to such a degree that he wished he was dead, repeatedly attempted to drown himself in his bath, and called for "the cyanide intended for him". The delusions gradually assumed a mystical, religious character, as he maintained direct relations with God, was a plaything of the devils, saw "miraculous apparitions", heard "holy music", and finally even believed he must be in another world.'

We might add that he cursed various people he took to be pursuing and disadvantaging him, foremost among them his erstwhile doctor Flechsig, whom he called a 'soul-murderer' while, on countless occasions, crying out 'little Flechsig', with a pronounced emphasis on the first word (p. 383). In June 1894, after a short stay elsewhere, he had come from Leipzig to the Sonnenstein Asylum near Pirna and stayed there until his condition was fully developed. In the course of the following years the clinical picture changed in a way best described in the words of the director of the asylum, Dr Weber:

'Without going into any further details as to the course of the illness, suffice it to say that, from the initial, more acute psychosis, which had a deleterious effect on the whole psychic process and can be categorized as hallucinatory insanity, what became increasingly dominant, what as it were came to crystallize, was the clinical picture of paranoia that now faces us' (p. 385). For, on the one hand, he had developed an artful delusional construction that we have every reason to find of interest, and, on the other, his personality had reconstructed itself and shown itself, apart from the odd disturbance, capable of dealing with the demands of life.

In his Assessment of 1899, Dr Weber reports as follows:

'At the present time, setting aside the psychomotor symptoms that would strike even the fleeting observer as pathological, Justice Dr Schreber appears, then, neither confused nor subject to psychical inhibition, nor of materially diminished intelligence; he is thoughtful; his memory is excellent; he has a considerable measure of knowledge, ranging beyond things juridical to many other domains, and is able to reproduce this in an orderly train of thought; he is interested in politics, science, art, etc., and is constantly occupied with them; and, in the aforementioned directions he would not betray much that might seem unusual to an observer not apprised of his general condition. Yet the patient is consumed by pathologically conditioned ideas, which have come together as a complete system, are more or less fixed as such, and appear not to be susceptible to correction by means of any objective appreciation and judgement of the actual state of things' (pp. 385–6).

Thus transformed, the patient believed himself to be capable of life's demands and undertook steps to effect the lifting of his guardian-ship order and discharge from the asylum. Dr Weber resisted these wishes and submitted reports in opposition to them; and yet, in an Assessment of 1900, he cannot help but depict the patient's nature and behaviour with some appreciation, in the following terms: 'The undersigned has, during meals shared at the family table over the course of nine months, had the most extensive opportunities to talk to Justice Schreber about all manner of things. Whatever came to be discussed – with the obvious exception of his delusions – whether it touched upon what went on in the domain of government and the law, politics, art and literature, the life of society, or what you will, Dr Schreber everywhere showed lively interest, knowledgeable insights, a good memory, perceptive judgement, and in ethical matters too an understanding that could only be commended. Equally, he behaved in a nice and friendly manner in his light banter with the ladies present and, where he treated certain things with humour, he remained tactful and decent, never drawing into our harmless talk at table the dis-cussion of matters that were to be dealt with in medical consultations rather than there' (pp. 397–8). He even came to intervene, in a pro-fessional and appropriate manner, in a business affair that affected the interests of the whole family (pp. 401 and 510).

In the repeated submissions to the court, through which Dr Schreber struggled for his release, he by no means denied his delusion and made no secret of his intention to publish the *Memoirs*. Rather, he stressed the value of his trains of thought for religious life and their invulnerability to critical attack by modern science; at the same time he insisted on the absolute harmlessness (p. 430) of all those actions to which he had been moved by the content of his delusion. The perspicacity and unswerving logic of one recognized as a paranoiac duly led to his triumph. In July 1902 Dr Schreber's guardianship order was lifted, and in the following year the *Memoirs of a Nervous Illness* appeared as a book, albeit in censored form, pruned of various valuable contents.

In the judgement that gave Dr Schreber back his freedom, the content of his delusional system is summed up in a few sentences: 'He takes himself to be called to redeem the world and to restore to it its lost bliss. But this he can only do if he has first transformed himself from a man into a woman' (p. 475).

For a comprehensive depiction of the delusion in its fully developed form we can turn to the Assessment supplied by Dr Weber in 1899: 'The patient's delusional system culminates in the idea that he has been called to bring salvation to the world and restore to humanity its lost bliss. He claims to have come to this mission by way of direct instructions from God, much as we are taught that the Prophets were. Precisely nerves in such a state of excitement as his had been for so long, were, he said, capable of attracting God; but these things could barely, if at all, be described in human language because they lay beyond the pale of human experience and were revealed to him alone. The essential prerequisite of his mission of salvation was his *transformation into a woman*. This was not to say that he *wished* to be thus transformed; it was rather a case of an imperative, grounded in the World Order, which he could ill escape, even if he would personally much rather have remained in his honourable masculine station in life; but the life of the beyond was to be won back for him and all mankind only by means of his transformation into a woman through divine miracles, which might lie years or even decades hence. He was, without a shadow of a doubt, the exclusive object of divine miracles, and so the most extraordinary human being ever to have lived on earth, miracles that he had experienced physically every minute of every hour over a period of years, and that were confirmed by the voices that spoke with him. In the first years of his illness he had been subject to the sort of damage to various organs of his body that would have quickly been the death of any other mortal, and so had lived for years without a stomach, without intestines, almost without lungs, with an oesophagus in shreds, with no bladder, with smashed rib bones, had sometimes eaten part of his larynx with his food, and so on, but divine miracles ("rays") had always repaired what had been destroyed, and so, for as long as he remained a man, he was quite immortal. Those menacing apparitions had now long disappeared, but in their stead his "femininity" had come to the fore, though this was a process of development that would probably take decades, if not centuries, to achieve, and whose end would not easily be experienced by anybody alive today. He had the feeling that large masses of "female nerves" had already passed over into his body, which would produce new humans through direct fertilization by God. Only then would he be able to die a natural death and to have gained bliss once more for himself as for all of mankind. In the meantime not only the sun, but also the trees and the birds, which were something akin to "the bemiracled remains of earlier human souls", spoke in human sounds to him, and wondrous things came to pass all around him' (pp. 386–8).

The interest of the practising psychiatrist in such delusional formations is typically exhausted once he has established the effects of the delusion and its influence on the patient's day-to-day existence; for him, wonder is not what lies at the root of understanding. The psychoanalyst derives from his knowledge of the psychoneuroses the supposition that even such peculiar trains of thought, so remote from habitual human thinking, have in fact emerged from the most general and comprehensible of emotions in the life of the soul, and so seeks to acquaint himself with the motives of, and the paths taken by, this transformation. With this intention, he will be glad to delve further into the details of the delusion and the history of its development.

a) The two main points stressed by the medical assessor are the *role of Redeemer* and the *transformation into a woman*. The Redeemer delusion is a fantasy familiar to us, given that it is frequently at the core of religious paranoia. The additional feature, that the redemption must follow from the transformation into a woman, is unusual and causes consternation in as far as it leads us well away from the historical myth that the patient's fantasy seeks to reproduce. It seems plausible that we should concur with the doctor's judgement that the ambition to play the role of Redeemer is the driving force of this delusional complex, while the *emasculation* can lay claim only to functioning as the means to this end. If this is how things appear in the final form of the delusion, however, our study of the *Memoirs* brings a quite different understanding to bear. We learn that the transformation into a woman (emasculation) was the primary delusion, which was at first adjudged to be an act of grievous impairment and persecution and came to be related to the role of Redeemer only on a secondary level. It is also beyond doubt that it was at first misused for sexual purposes rather than serving higher designs. To put this in formal terms, what was for the patient a delusion of sexual persecution was retroactively transformed into religious megalomania. The persecutor was initially taken to be the patient's doctor, Prof. Flechsig, with God Himself taking his place in due course.

Let me present here in unabridged form those sections of the *Memoirs* that show this to be the case: 'In this way a plot was hatched against me (around March or April 1894), which, following the recognition, or the assumption, that my nervous illness was incurable, aimed to hand me over to a certain person in such a way as to relinquish my soul to him, but to have my body – this, in a mistaken apprehension of the above-mentioned tendencies that underpin the World Order – transformed into a female body and, as such, abandoned to the person in question for the purpose of sexual abuse,[3] before being simply "left lying there", that is, no doubt, abandoned to decay' (p. 56).

'From the human point of view that then still held sway over me, it was here quite natural that I should only see Professor Flechsig or his soul as my real enemy (and later the soul of v. W., as we will see below) and the omnipotence of God as my natural ally, which I fancied to be in distress only when confronted by Professor Flechsig and so to have to be supported by all imaginable means, even to the extent of sacrificing myself. That God Himself could be, if not the initiator, then at least well aware of the plan to commit soul-murder upon me and to abandon my body as a female harlot, is an idea that came upon me only much later, indeed that, I might venture, has in part become clear to me only during the writing of the present essay' (p. 59).

'Of all the attempts at soul-murder, at emasculation for purposes *contrary to the World Order*[34] (that is, for the satisfaction of a person's sexual desires), and later at the destruction of my mind, none has succeeded. Though I have much bitter suffering and hardship behind me, I emerge from the apparently so unequal fight between a single weak human being and God Himself as victor, because I have the World Order on my side' (p. 61).

In note 34[4] the later reconfiguration of the delusion of emasculation and of the relationship to God is announced: 'The fact that emasculation for another purpose, one *consonant* with the World Order, lies within the realms of possibility, indeed that it may contain the probable resolution of the conflict, will be addressed in detail later.'

These comments are of decisive importance for our understanding of the delusion of emasculation and so of the case as a whole. We might add that the 'voices' that the patient heard always treated the transformation into a woman as a cause for sexual shame, giving them grounds for scorning him. 'In view of my apparently imminent emasculation as *"Miss Schreber"*, rays of God[5] often felt able to make a mockery of me' (p. 127). – 'And this individual who lets himself be f . . . . d[6] calls himself a one-time Presiding Judge?' – 'Aren't you ashamed to face your lady wife?'

The primary nature of the emasculation fantasy and its initial independence from the idea of the Redeemer are further illustrated by the 'notion' mentioned at the start that occurred to him while half asleep, namely, that it must be a nice thing to be a woman undergoing intercourse (p. 36). The awareness of this fantasy dates back to the incubation period of the illness, that is, before the effects of the excessive workload in Dresden.

The month of November 1895 is deemed by Schreber himself to be the time in which the connection between the fantasy of emasculation and the idea of the Redeemer established itself and thus a reconciliation with the former was set in motion. 'But now I came to see beyond any doubt that the World Order simply demanded this emasculation, whether it suited me personally or not, and that *reason* dictated that I had no choice but to reconcile myself with the thought of being transformed into a woman. The only possible result of the emasculation was, of course, fertilization by the divine rays with the purpose of creating new human beings' (p. 177).

The transformation into a woman was the *punctum saliens*, the initial seed for the formation of the delusion; it also proved to be the only element that survived his recovery and the only one that claimed its place in the patient's real actions when he was restored to health. 'The *only thing* that may appear to be unreasonable in the eyes of other people is the fact, also touched upon by the expert witness, that I am on occasion discovered standing before the mirror or elsewhere with certain feminine adornments (ribbons, costume necklaces, and the like), my torso half naked. It should be said that this occurs only when I am *alone*, never, if I can avoid it, where others might see me' (p. 429). The Presiding Judge admitted to toying in this way at a time (July 1901) when he found the true way of expressing the recovery of his health for practical purposes: 'I have now long realized that the persons I see before me are not "fleetingly improvised men" but real human beings, and that I thus have to behave in relation to them as a reasonable human being is wont to do in his dealings with others' (p. 409). In contrast with this active implementation of the emasculation fantasy, the patient never sought the acknowledgement of his mission as Redeemer other than through the publication of his *Memoirs*.

b) The relationship of our patient to *God* is so peculiar, so full of contradictory determinants, that it is only with a dose of good faith that we can hold on to the expectation of finding 'method' in this 'madness'. We must now turn for help to what is said in the *Memoirs* in order to achieve a clearer orientation in the at once theological and psychological system of Dr Schreber and to set out in their seeming (delusional) connection his views on the *nerves,* on *bliss,* on the *divine hierarchy,* and the *qualities of God*. In all parts of the theory, we are struck by the curious mixture of banality and cleverness, of borrowed and original elements.

The human soul is contained within the *nerves* of the body, which are conceived of as a structure of extraordinary finesse – comparable to the finest of threads. Certain of these nerves are suitable only for the registration of sensory perceptions, others (*the intelligence nerves*) are responsible for everything psychical, according to the principle that *each individual intelligence nerve represents the complete mental individuality of the human being* and the greater or lesser number of the intelligence nerves present influences only the period of time for which the impressions can be held fast.[7]

While humans consist of body and nerves, God is inherently nothing but nerve. The nerves of God are not, however, limited in number, as in the human body, but infinite or eternal. They possess all the attributes of human nerves on an enormously increased scale. In their capacity to create, that is to convert themselves into all possible things in the created world, they are called *rays*. Between God and the firmament or the sun there exists an intimate relation.[8]

After the work of creation God retreated to a great distance (pp. 10–11 and 252) and generally left the world to its own laws. He limited Himself to drawing up to Him the souls of the dead. Only by way of exception might He establish contact with highly talented individuals,[9] or intervene through a miracle in the destinies of the world. A regular intercourse between God and human souls occurs, according to the World Order, only after death.[10] When a person has died, the parts of his soul (nerves) are subjected to a process of purification, in order finally to be reattributed to God Himself as 'forecourts of Heaven'. There thus arises an eternal circulation of things, which is the basis of the World Order. When God creates something, He emits a part of Himself, giving another shape to one part of His nerves. The loss that thereby appears to arise is in its turn restored when, after hundreds and thousands of years, the nerves of the deceased enter into bliss and so accrue back to Him as 'forecourts of Heaven' (pp. 18 and 19 n.).

The souls that have been cleansed by the process of purification enjoy a state of *bliss*.[11] In the meantime they have weakened their consciousness of self and merged with other souls into higher entities. Notable souls, like those of Goethe, Bismarck, etc., must perhaps preserve their sense of identity for centuries before they can in their turn be incorporated by higher complexes of souls (such as 'rays of Jehovah' for ancient Jewry and 'rays of Zoroaster' for the Persians). During the purification the souls learn 'the language spoken by God Himself, the so-called "elementary language", a somewhat archaic but none the less powerful German, which was especially distinguished by a great wealth of euphemisms' (p. 13).[12] God Himself is no simple entity. 'Above the "forecourts of Heaven" God Himself floated, who, in contrast to these "frontal realms of God", is also known as the "rear realms of God". The rear realms of God were subject (and are subject still) to a peculiar division, whereby a lower God (Ahriman) and an upper God (Ormazd) were distinguished' (p. 19). Schreber can say nothing more about the significance of this division than that the lower God tended to be more inclined towards peoples of the darker race (the Semites) and the upper towards the blond peoples (Aryans). This is the limit, though, of what might be expected of human knowledge at such heights. We none the less also learn that, 'in spite of the unity of God's omnipotence, which must in some sense be sustained', the lower and the upper God 'have to be conceived as distinct entities, both of which, *also in relationship to each other,* are possessed of their own particular egoism and their particular drive for self-preservation, and so always seek by turns to get the upper hand' (p. 140 n.). The two divine entities also behaved in quite different ways towards the unfortunate Schreber during the acute stage of his illness.[13]

Justice Schreber was in his healthy days a sceptic in matters religious (pp. 29 and 64); he had not been able to attain to a firm faith in the existence of a personal God. Indeed, he derives from this fact of his previous history an argument serving to support the full reality of his delusion.[14] Anybody, however, who comes to know the following details of the characteristics of Schreber's God, will surely aver that the transformation brought about by the paranoid illness was not especially thoroughgoing in nature and that in what is now a Redeemer there remains much of the erstwhile sceptic.

For there is a gap in the World Order, as a result of which the very existence of God appears to be under threat. By virtue of an

15

inscrutable connection, the nerves of *living* people, more especially when these are in a state of *high-level arousal,* exert such a powerful attraction upon the nerves of God that He can no longer free Himself from them, so that His own existence is threatened (p. 11). This extraordinarily rare event, then, came about for Schreber and brought with it the greatest sufferings for him. God's drive for self-preservation was aroused by this (p. 30), and it became evident that God is far removed from the perfection that religions ascribe to Him. Throughout Schreber's entire book runs the bitter accusa-tion that, being accustomed only to relations with the dead, God *does not comprehend the living.*

'Yet a *fundamental misapprehension* obtains here, which has since run through my entire life like a red thread and which lies in the fact that, *according to the World Order, God did not know the living* and had no need of doing so, but followed the World Order in having relations only with corpses' (p. 55). – 'That this is so must, I feel certain, in its turn be linked to the fact that God had no idea of how to relate to living people and was accustomed only to relations with corpses or with persons lying asleep (in dream)' (p. 141). – '*Incredibile scriptu,* I myself am tempted to add, and yet all of this is in fact true, as imposs-ible as it may be for others to grasp the notion of God's utter incapability of judging living people correctly, and as long as it has taken me to come to terms with this thought after all the innumerable observations I have made on this matter' (p. 246).

It is only as a result of God's misunderstanding of the living that He Himself could come to instigate the plot against Schreber, that God could take him to be stupid and set him the most arduous trials (p. 264). He submitted to a highly irksome form of 'compulsive thinking' in order to escape this condemnation. 'Whenever my thought processes cease, God immediately considers my mental abilities to be extinguished, He sees confirmed the destruction of my intellect that He had hoped for (stupidity), and with it the possibility of withdrawal' (p. 206).

God's behaviour in the matter of the urge to defecate, or sh . . , provokes an especially intense sense of outrage. So characteristic is the passage that I will cite it in full. An understanding of this depends on the realization that both the miracles and the voices are derived from God (that is, from the divine rays).

'Because of its characteristic significance, I must devote some additional remarks to the aforementioned question "Why don't you sh . . , then?", however indecent the theme on which I am thereby forced to touch. Like everything else to do with my body, the need to defecate is prompted by miracles; this comes about by the faeces being pushed forwards in the intestine (and sometimes backwards again), and if, owing to other recent evacuations, sufficient material is no longer available, the few remaining remnants of the contents of the intestine at least are smeared on my anal orifice. This is a miracle of the upper God, which is repeated at least several dozen times each day. Connected with this is an idea beyond human comprehension and only to be explained by virtue of God's total lack of knowledge of living humans as organisms, namely that "sh . . . ing" is so to speak the last thing, so that by miracling up the urge to sh . . the aim of destroying the intellect is achieved and the possibility of a definitive withdrawal is given to the rays. It seems to me that, in order fundamentally to grasp how this idea comes into being, one must conceive of the presence of a misapprehension as to the symbolic meaning of the act of defecation, namely that one who has come to relate to the divine rays to the extent that I have is in a certain sense entitled to sh . . on the whole world.

'At the same time, however, this is an expression of the complete perfidiousness of the politics being pursued against me.[15] Almost invariably when the urge to defecate is miracled upon me, some other person from those around me is sent – by means of exciting their nerves – to the lavatory, in order to prevent me from defecating; this is a phenomenon that I have observed over the years on such a regular basis and on such innumerable occasions (running into the thousands) that any notion of coincidence can be ruled out. When I am then asked the question "Why don't you sh . . , then?" the admirable answer follows: "Maybe because I'm stupid." My pen almost baulks at writing such arrant nonsense as that God, in the blindness that springs from His ignorance of human nature, can indeed go as far as to assume that a human being might exist who, unlike even the animals, is unable to sh . . out of stupidity. When I feel the necessity and actually defecate, generally using a bucket, as I almost invariably find the lavatory engaged, this is always accompanied by a most powerful emotion of voluptuousness of the soul. For the liberation from the pressure caused by the faeces present in the intestine leads to an intensive sense of well-being for the nerves of voluptuousness; the same is true of pissing. For this reason it has on each occasion been the case that all the rays are united during defecation or pissing. It is precisely for this reason that when I am about to execute these natural functions an attempt is always made, albeit generally without success, to reverse-miracle the urge to defecate or to piss' (pp. 225–7).[16]

Schreber's strange God is also not capable of learning from experience: 'To derive a lesson for the future from the experience gained here seems to be prevented by certain characteristics intrinsic to the nature of God' (p. 186). He can thus repeat without variation the same torturous trials, miracles and utterances of voices over a period of years, so that He becomes an object of derision for the victim of His persecution.

'So it is that, in almost everything that happens to me, God for the most part comes to appear ridiculous or childish once the miracles have to a large extent lost their erstwhile terror for me. The effect of this for my behaviour is that I am frequently forced in self-defence to play the role of *God's mocker*, and this, if I am so disposed, at the top of my voice . . .' (p. 333).[17]

This criticism of God and resistance to Him is, however, met in Schreber by an energetic counter-current to which he gives vent at numerous points: 'Here I must, however, stress in the most decisive fashion that this is but an episode that will, I trust, come to an end when I am deceased, if not before, and that the right to mock God is thus granted only to me and to no other. For other people God remains the omnipotent Creator of Heaven and earth, the root cause of all things and their future salvation, to whom, even if certain of the traditional religious ideas are in need of correction, worship and the utmost reverence are due' (pp. 333–4).

So, repeated attempts are made to justify the behaviour of God towards the patient, showing all the ingenuity that theodicies are wont to do, as he one moment cites the general nature of souls, the next God's need to preserve Himself and the deceptive influence of the Flechsig soul (pp. 60–61 and 160). On the whole, though, the illness is conceived of as a struggle of Schreber the man against God, where the weak human prevails because he has the World Order on his side (p. 61).

From the medical reports one might easily conclude that in the case of Schreber one is dealing with the common form of the Redeemer fantasy, with the patient as son of God, destined to save the world from its misery or from the demise with which it is threatened, and so on. I have thus not spared the detail of the particular features of Schreber's relationship to God. The importance of this relationship for the rest of humankind is rarely mentioned in the *Memoirs* and only when the formation of the delusion is complete. It essentially consists in the impossibility of any dead person finding bliss as long as his (Schreber's) person attracts to itself and absorbs the greater mass of the divine rays. The undisguised identification with Jesus Christ also emerges only at a very late stage (pp. 338 and 431).

Any attempt to explain the Schreber Case that fails to give these peculiarities of his conception of God, this mixture of traits of reverence and resistance, their due cannot hope to achieve the truth. Let us now turn to another theme that is intimately bound up with God, that of *bliss*.

For Schreber bliss is also 'the life beyond', to which the human soul is raised by purification after death. He describes it as a condition of uninterrupted enjoyment, connected to the contemplation of God. This is not particularly original in itself, but we are surprised by the distinction that Schreber draws between a male and a female state of bliss. 'Male bliss had higher status than did the female equivalent, which appears to have consisted above all in an uninterrupted feeling of voluptuousness' (p. 18).[18] Other passages announce the coinciding of bliss and voluptuousness in clearer terms and without reference to sexual difference, just as that component of bliss which is the contemplation of God is no longer dealt with. Thus, for example:

'. . . with the nature of the nerves of God, by dint of which bliss . . . if not exclusively, is at least in some part a heightened sensation of voluptuousness' (p. 51). And again: 'Voluptuousness can be understood as a foretaste of the state of bliss, granted to humans and to other living beings, as it were in advance' (p. 281), so that heavenly bliss might essentially be understood as an intensification and continuation of earthly sensual pleasures!

It would be quite wrong to suppose that this conception of bliss is an element of the Schreber delusion derived from the first stages of the illness and later eliminated on grounds of incompatibility. As late as in the Statement of his Case (in July 1901) the patient draws attention to what he sees as one of his great insights: 'that voluptuousness indeed stands in a close relationship to the bliss of departed spirits, one as yet not recognizable to other humans'.[19]

Indeed, we will learn that this 'close relationship' is the rock on which the patient has built his hopes for an eventual reconciliation with God and an end to his suffering. The rays of God lose their antagonistic intentions as soon as they are guaranteed voluptuousness of the soul in being absorbed into his body (p. 133); God Himself desires to find voluptuousness in him (p. 283), and threatens to retract His rays if he neglects the maintenance of his voluptuousness and cannot offer God what He desires (p. 320).

This surprising sexualization of heavenly blissfulness gives us the impression that Schreber's concept of bliss (*Seligkeit*) has arisen out of a condensation of the two main meanings of the German word *selig*: 'deceased' and 'sensually happy'.[20] We will, however, also find here occasion for submitting to scrutiny our patient's relationship to eroticism as a whole, to questions of sexual enjoyment, for we psychoanalysts have to date embraced the opinion that the roots of every nervous and psychic illness are chiefly to be found in the domain of sexual life, some of us from reasons of experience alone, others also as a result of theoretical considerations.

On the basis of the samples of the Schreber delusion given thus far, we can dismiss the concern that this paranoid illness could emerge as the 'negative case' so long sought for, where sexuality plays an all too minor role. Schreber himself expresses himself on countless occasions in the manner of a follower of our prejudice. He always speaks of 'nervosity' and erotic lapses in the same breath, as if the two were inseparable.[21]

Before falling ill, Justice Schreber was a man of strict morals: 'There can be few people' – he claims, and I see no justification for doubting him – 'who have been raised according to such strict moral principles as I, and who have their whole life long, not least in sexual matters, adopted a reservation in keeping with these principles to the extent that I can claim to have done' (p. 281). After the severe spiritual struggle, which was outwardly manifest in the symptoms of the illness, the relationship to the erotic had changed. He had come to the perception that the maintenance of voluptuousness was his duty, and that its fulfilment was the only way of ending the severe conflict that had broken out within or, as he thought, about him. Voluptuousness had become 'God-fearing', so the voices assured him (p. 285), and he regrets only that he is not in a position to devote himself all day long to its maintenance (loc. cit.).[22]

That, then, was the result of the changes in Schreber caused by his illness in terms of the two principal directions of his delusion. Before, he was inclined towards sexual asceticism and was a doubter with regard to God, while after the illness had taken its course, he became a believer in God and devoted to voluptuousness. But, just as his regained faith in God was of a peculiar kind, so the element of sexual enjoyment that he had conquered for himself had a very strange character. It was no longer the sexual freedom of the male, but feminine sexual feeling; he took up a feminine position with regard to God, feeling himself to be the wife of God.[23]

No other part of his delusion is treated so thoroughly, even persistently, as his ostensible transformation into a woman. The nerves he absorbed assumed the character of the nerves of female voluptuousness in his body and gave it in other ways a more or less feminine stamp, in particular by lending his skin the softness that is peculiar to the female sex (p. 87). When he exerts gentle pressure with his hand on a random part of the body, he can feel these nerves beneath the surface of the skin as a formation of thread-like or stringy nature, not least in the chest where women have their breasts. 'By exerting pressure on this formation, and especially while thinking of something feminine, I am able to attain a sensation of voluptuousness that corresponds to that of women' (p. 277). He has no doubt that this formation is in origin nothing other than erstwhile nerves of God, which in their transfer to his body can hardly have forfeited their quality as nerves (p. 279). By means of what he calls 'drawing' (visual imagining) he is able to give both himself and the rays the impression that his body is fitted with female breasts and female genitals: 'The drawing of a female bottom on my body – *honi soit qui mal y pense* – has become such a habit that I do it almost involuntarily each time I bend over' (p. 233). He wishes 'boldly to claim that anybody who might see me standing before the mirror with the upper part of my torso bared – especially if the illusion is supported by some feminine ornament – would be bound to conceive of it as a *female bust*' (p. 280). He calls for a medical examination to confirm that his entire body from top to toe is pervaded by nerves of voluptuousness, which he believes to be the case only in the female body, while for men, as far as he is aware, the nerves of voluptuousness are to be found only in the sexual organ and its immediate surroundings (p. 274). The voluptuousness of the soul that has developed through this accumulation of nerves in his body is so powerful that, in particular when he is lying in bed, it takes only a slight effort of the imagination for him to achieve sensual pleasure, giving a fairly clear premonition of the sexual pleasure a woman feels in intercourse (p. 269).

If we recall the dream that occurred during the incubation period of his illness, before the move to Dresden, then there can be no doubt that the delusion of his transformation into a woman is nothing other than the realization of the content of that dream. At that time he had resisted the dream with masculine indignation, and he also initially struggled against its fulfilment during the illness, viewing the transformation into a woman as a disgrace that was to be exacted of him through ill intent. A time arrived, however (in November 1895), when he began to come to terms with this transformation, connecting it with the more elevated intentions of God: 'Since then I have quite consciously inscribed the cultivation of femininity upon my banner' (pp. 177–8).

He then reached the firm conviction that God Himself demanded femininity from him for His own satisfaction:

'As soon, though – if I can put it in this way – that God and I are alone together, I feel the necessity to employ every possible means and all my mental resources, in particular my powers of imagination, to make the divine rays conceive of me as constantly as possible, or – this being beyond human capability – at least at certain times of the day, as a woman luxuriating in voluptuous feelings' (p. 281).

'God, on the other hand, in line with the conditions of existence of souls according to the World Order, demands a *continuous enjoyment*; it is my task to achieve this for Him . . . in the form of the most ample development of voluptuousness of the soul; in as far as I garner some sensual enjoyment I am entitled to take this with me as a small reimbursement for the excess of sufferings and sacrifices that has been imposed upon me for years now . . .' (p. 283).

'. . . on the basis of the impressions I have gained, I might even venture the view that God would never proceed to effect a withdrawal (a process that at first always leads to a considerable worsening of my bodily well-being), but would be led by the attraction without any resistance and in a constant fashion, if it were only possible for me *always* to play the woman lying in sexual embrace with myself, *always* to rest my gaze on female forms, *always* to view female images, and so forth' (pp. 284–5).

The two principal elements of Schreber's delusion, the transformation into a woman and the privileged relation to God, are linked up in his system by the feminine disposition towards God. An inevitable task for us will be to prove an essential, *genetic* relationship between these two elements; otherwise our elucidations of Schreber's delusion would lead us to play the role described by Kant in the famous image from the *Critique of Pure Reason* as that of the man who holds the sieve under a billy-goat while another milks it.

Notes

1. That is, the time before the effects of overwork in his new post, which he took to be to blame.

2. That is, at the Leipzig clinic of Prof. Flechsig.

3. The context of this and other passages shows that the person in question, who was to carry out the abuse, was none other than Flechsig (see below).

4. [Freud's gloss to Schreber's n. 34 above.]

5. The 'rays of God' are, as we shall see, identical with the voices that speak in the 'elementary language'.

6. As with all the other singularities of style, I copy this ellipsis from the *Memoirs*. Personally, I can see no reason to feel so shameful in a serious matter of this kind.

7. In the note on this theory, which is stressed by Schreber, its usefulness for the explanation of heredity is drawn out. 'The male seed contains one of the father's nerves and creates a new unity by combining with a nerve taken from the body of the mother' (p. 7). The characteristic that we would ascribe to the spermatozoon is thus transferred here to the nerves, suggesting that Schreber's 'nerves' probably derive from the realm of sexual ideas. It is not infrequently the case in the *Memoirs* that a passing note on a delusional theory contains the clue we seek as to the genesis and thus the significance of the delusion.

8. See also the discussion of the sun below. – The equivalence (or rather condensation) of nerves and rays may well be based on the linear appearance that they share. – The ray-nerves are, in any event, as creative as the sperm-nerves.

9. In the 'elementary language' (see below) this is denoted by the expression 'to take up nerve association with them'.

10. We will see later what objections against God are connected with this.

11. This essentially consists in a feeling of voluptuous pleasure (see below).

12. On only one occasion during his illness was the patient allowed to glimpse with his inner eye the omnipotence of God in its total purity. At that time God uttered a word that was routine in the elementary language, the expressive but hardly friendly 'Luder!' ['slut!'] (p. 136).

13. A note (20) suggests that the choice of the names of Persian deities is determined by a passage in Byron's *Manfred*. We will encounter the influence of this work once more below.

14. 'The suggestion that *my case* involves mere illusions seems to me to be inherently unthinkable from a psychological point of view. For the illusion that one is in communication with God or with the souls of the deceased can only properly come about in individuals who enter into their pathologically excited nervous state with a secure belief in God and in the immortality of the soul. *In my case this was not in any sense true, as the discussion at the beginning of the chapter made clear*' (p. 79).

15. A note at this point seeks to temper the harsh word 'perfidiousness' by referring to the justifications of God that will follow.

16. This admission of taking pleasure in excretion, which we have come to know as one of the auto-erotic components of infantile sexuality, might be seen in conjunction with the words of little Hans in the 'Analysis of a Phobia in a Five-year-old Boy' (1909) [II].

17. In the elementary language, too, God was not only the one who cursed but occasionally also subject to cursing, as, for example: 'Damn and blast, it's hard to say that the dear Lord lets himself be f . . . . d' (p. 194).

18. It is surely quite consonant with the wish-fulfilment of life in the hereafter that one should then finally be rid of sexual difference.

> *Und jene himmlischen Gestalten*
> *sie fragen nicht nach Mann und Weib.*
> (Mignon)

[And those heavenly figures, they ask not who is man or woman.]

19. For a discussion of the possible profundity of Schreber's finding, see below.

20. Extreme examples of the two meanings would be: 'my late father' ['Mein seliger Vater'], and the text of the aria from *Don Juan*:

> *Ja, dein zu sein auf ewig,*
> *wie selig werd' ich sein.*

[Yes, to be yours for ever, how blissful I will be.]

There must surely be some sense, though, in the fact that our language uses the same word for such different situations.

21. 'If on some world *moral rottenness* ("voluptuous excesses") *or perhaps also nervosity* had taken hold of the whole of humanity in this fashion' – then, says Schreber, after the model of the biblical reports of Sodom and

Gomorrah, of the Flood, etc., that world might have reached its catastrophic end (p. 52). – '[The story] . . . sowed fear and terror among people, destroyed the foundations of religion, and caused *a general nervosity and immorality* to spread widely, with devastating pestilences befalling humanity in their wake' (p. 91). 'The uncanny power that could develop as an enemy of God out of a *moral decay* of humanity *or out of general over-excitation of the nerves as a result of an excess of culture*, was thus probably what the souls meant by a "Prince of Hell" ' (p. 163).

22. In the context of the delusion we are told (pp. 179–80): 'The attraction lost its terror for the nerves in question, however, in as far as, when they entered my body, they encountered the feeling of voluptuousness of the soul, in which they shared in their turn. They thus found in my body a fully or virtually equivalent substitute for the heavenly bliss they had lost, which surely also consisted in an enjoyment akin to voluptuousness.'

23. A note to the Preface (4) reads: 'Something has happened to my body that is much like the conception of Jesus Christ on the part of an immaculate virgin – a woman, that is, who has never entertained relations with a man. On two separate occasions (this, in the period when I was still in Flechsig's institution) I had, albeit somewhat underdeveloped, female genitals and felt movements in my body such as are caused by the first stirring into life of the human embryo: through a divine miracle the nerves of God had been cast into my body like the male seed, and a fertilization had thus taken place.'

II

Attempts at Interpretation

There are two possible angles for an attempt at pressing forward towards an understanding of this case history of paranoia and uncovering the familiar complexes and driving forces of the life of the soul: that of the delusional remarks of the patient himself or that of the factors which prompted his illness.

The first path would seem attractive since C. G. Jung provided us with the brilliant example of the interpretation of a much more severe case of dementia praecox and one with symptomatic manifestations far more remote from the normal.[1] The high degree of intelligence in the patient and his readiness to communicate seem to alleviate the difficulty of resolving the task by following this path. He not infrequently hands us the key himself by the apparently casual addition of an elucidation, a quotation, or an example to one of his delusional propositions, or by expressly contesting a similarity that has dawned on him. In this last case, one has only to follow the familiar psychoanalytic technique of dispensing with negative appearances, taking the example as the real substance, the quotation or the corroboration as the source, and one finds oneself in possession of the sought-after translation from the paranoid form of expression into the normal. It might be worthwhile to represent an example of this technique in more detail. Schreber complains about the nuisance of the so-called 'miracled birds' or 'speaking birds', to which he ascribes a whole series of quite striking characteristics (pp. 208–14). It is his conviction that they are fashioned out of remnants of former 'forecourts of Heaven', that is, out of human souls which have found bliss, and have been set upon him, loaded with cadaveric poison. They have been conditioned to recite 'senseless figures of speech, learned by rote', which have been 'drummed into' them. On each occasion when they have unloaded their cadaveric poison on to him, i.e., 'reeled off the phrases that have, as it were, been drummed into them', they come to be in some sense absorbed into his soul, with the words 'damned fellow' or 'damn it!', the only words that they are still able to utter with real feeling. They do not understand the words they speak but they do have a natural receptivity for the harmony of sounds, whether total or partial. They are thus unconcerned whether one says:

> '*Santiago*' or '*Karthago*'
> '*Chinesentum*' or '*Jesum Christum*'
> '*Abendrot*' or '*Atemnot*'
> '*Ariman*' or '*Ackermann*', etc. (p. 210).

['Santiago' or 'Carthage'/'Chinese-dom' or 'Jesus Christum'/'Sunset' or 'Breathlessness'/'Ahriman' or 'Husbandman.']

As one reads this description one cannot but think that what are meant here are young girls, who – when we are in a critical mood – are readily compared with geese, to whom we in a less than gallant fashion ascribe a 'bird-brain', and of whom we claim that they can say only the phrases they have been taught to say and that they betray their lack of cultivation by the confusion of similar-sounding foreign words. The 'damned fellow' who is the only thing they take seriously would then represent the triumph of the young man who has managed to impress them. And, lo and behold, a few pages further on one comes upon the sentences of Schreber's that put this interpretation beyond doubt. 'I jokingly applied girls' names to a great number of the remaining bird-souls in order to distinguish them, as, with their curiosity, their voluptuous inclinations, etc., they are all most readily comparable to little girls. These girls' names were subsequently adopted in part by the divine rays and retained in order to denote the respective bird-souls.' From this easily achieved interpretation of the 'miracled birds' a clue to the understanding of the enigmatic 'forecourts of Heaven' can be derived.

I am well aware that a good dose of tact and restraint is required in psychoanalytic work when we leave the typical cases of interpretation behind and that the listener or reader will go only as far as the familiarity he has achieved with analytical techniques allows. There is thus every reason to be wary of allowing an increased level of ingenuity to be accompanied by a reduced measure of certainty and trustworthiness. It is only natural that one analyst will err in his work on the side of caution, another on the side of audacity. It will be possible to demarcate the correct boundaries of what is justified in interpretation only after manyifold attempts and an improved acquaintance with the subject. In my work on the Schreber Case, restraint is prescribed by the fact that attempts to resist the publication of the *Memoirs* have been successful in removing from our knowledge a considerable part of the material and probably that part which would be of most significance for our understanding.[2] This is the case, for instance, with the ending of Chapter III of the book, which started out with the highly promising announcement: 'I will first deal with certain events experienced by *other members of my family*, which might well be related to the soul-murder as postulated and which at any rate all carry a mysterious stamp, one not to be explained in terms of ordinary human experience' (p. 33) and immediately followed it with the sentence: 'The remaining content of the chapter is deemed unsuitable for publication and is excised.' I shall therefore have to be content if I am successful in tracing with a degree of certainty the core at least of the delusional structure back to its origin in familiar human motivation.

With this aim I will thus add in a small part of the case history that is not sufficiently acknowledged in the assessments, in spite of the fact that the patient did all he could to put it to the fore. I am referring here to Schreber's relationship with his first doctor, Privy Councillor Prof. Flechsig of Leipzig.

We already know that the Schreber Case initially fitted the mould of the delusion of persecution, and that this became obscured only after the turning-point of the illness (the 'reconciliation'). The persecutions then become increasingly bearable; the purpose of the threatened emasculation in terms of the World Order caused the sense of disgrace to recede. The origin of all the persecutions, though, is Flechsig, and he remains their instigator throughout the course of the illness.[3]

The nature of Flechsig's atrocity and of what motives might have driven him to it is narrated in that characteristically vague and elusive fashion that can be viewed as a mark of the particularly intensive elaboration of a delusion, if we can judge paranoia after the model of the much more familiar case of dreams. Flechsig committed soul-murder on his patient, or at least sought to, an act that might be compared to the efforts of the Devil and of demons to take control of his soul and which was perhaps prefigured in dealings between long-deceased members of the Flechsig and Schreber families (pp. 22ff.). It would be desirable to find out more about the meaning of this soul-murder, but the sources once more have a tendentious way of failing us here: 'As to the precise nature of the soul-murder and, as it were, its technique, I am unable to expand on what I have intimated above. The only thing I would add is (there follows a section that is unsuitable for publication)' (p. 28). As a result of this omission what is intended by 'soul-murder' remains obscure to us. The only clue that escaped censorship will be mentioned further on.

Whatever the case, a further development of the delusion soon followed, which affected the patient's relationship to God, but not to Flechsig. If he had hitherto perceived a real enemy only in Flechsig (or rather in his soul) and viewed God's omnipotence as his ally, he could now not shake off the thought that God Himself was complicit in, if not the instigator of, the plan drawn up against him (p. 59). Flechsig, however, remained the first seducer, and God subject to his influence (p. 60). He had found the means to launch himself with all his soul, or at least part of it, into Heaven and – without undergoing death and preparatory cleansing – to make of himself the 'leader of the rays' (p. 56).[4] The Flechsig soul retained this role, even when the patient had moved from the Leipzig clinic to Pierson's asylum. The influence of the new surroundings showed itself in the fact that the soul of the chief orderly, recognized by the patient as somebody who had formerly lived in the same house, joined Flechsig's as the soul of von W.[5] The Flechsig soul then

introduced the 'division of souls', which took on considerable pro-
portions. At one particular time there were between 40 and 60 such
fractions of the Flechsig soul; two larger parts of the soul were
known as the 'upper Flechsig' and the 'middle Flechsig'. The von
W. soul (that of the chief orderly) behaved in the same way (p. 111).
It could be quite comical to see the two souls feuding in spite of
their alliance, through the mutual repulsion of the aristocratic pride
of the one and the professorial arrogance of the other (p. 113). In
the first weeks of his final stay at Sonnenstein (in the summer of
1894) the soul of the new psychiatrist, Dr Weber, came into play,
and soon after there arose that reversal in the development of his
delusion that we have come to know as the 'reconciliation'.

During the later stay at Sonnenstein, when God began to give the
patient more of his due, there was a raid on the souls, which had
infuriatingly multiplied, so that the Flechsig soul remained in just
one or two forms and the von W. soul in a single one. The latter
soon disappeared altogether; the Flechsig soul elements, which
gradually declined in their intelligence and power, then came to be
known as the 'rear Flechsig' and the 'Well-then-party'. We know
from the Preface, the 'Open Letter to Privy Councillor Prof. Dr
Flechsig', that the Flechsig soul retained its significance to the end.

This curious document expresses the certain conviction that the
doctor who is influencing him has himself had the same visions as
the patient and received the same disclosures in transcendental
matters, and it insists from the start that the author of the *Memoirs*
has not the least intention of attacking the doctor's honour. This is
reiterated earnestly and emphatically in the patient's submissions
(pp. 343 and 445); we can see that he is seeking to separate 'Flechsig
the soul' from the living person of this name, the delusional Flechsig
from the physical.[6]

Having studied a series of cases of delusion of persecution, I, and
also others, have developed the impression that the relationship of
the patient to his persecutor can be solved according to a simple
formula.[7] The person to whom the delusion ascribes such great
power and influence and in whose hands all the threads of the

conspiracy are brought together is, if given a specific identity, the same one as was of no less importance for the emotional life of the patient before the onset of the illness or an easily recognized surrogate. The emotional importance is projected in the shape of an external power, the tone of the emotion turned into its opposite; the individual now hated and feared as a result of his persecution was once loved and admired. The persecution established by the delusion serves above all to justify the patient's emotional transformation.

With this view in mind, let us consider the relations that had earlier existed between the patient and his physician and persecutor, Flechsig. We already know that in the years 1884 and 1885 Schreber negotiated a first nervous illness that ran its course 'without any occurrences bordering on the transcendental domain' (p. 35). During this condition, described as 'hypochondria', which apparently stayed within the bounds of a neurosis, Flechsig was the patient's doctor. Schreber spent six months at the Leipzig University Clinic at this time. We are told that after his recovery he remembered his doctor in positive terms. 'The main thing was that, after a lengthy convalescent journey, I was cured, and I could therefore be filled only with a lively sense of gratitude towards Prof. Flechsig at that time, which I particularly emphasized by visiting him later and paying him what I considered to be an appropriate fee.' It is true that in the *Memoirs* Schreber's praise of his first treatment by Flechsig is not delivered without certain caveats, but this may well be understood by the fact that his attitude towards him has in the meantime diametrically changed. The remark that follows on from that just cited suggests the original warmth of feeling for the successful doctor: 'The gratitude was perhaps still more heartfelt on the part of my wife, who revered Prof. Flechsig as the man who had no less than restored her husband to her, so that years later his picture was still standing on her desk' (p. 36).

As we are denied any insight into the causes of the first bout of illness, the understanding of which would doubtless be of vital importance for the elucidation of the second, grave illness, we must hope for serendipity as we grasp at a matter unknown to us. We know that in the incubation period of the illness (between his

appointment and the taking up of office, from June to October 1893)
there were recurrent dreams in which the earlier nervous illness
had apparently returned. When he was once half asleep he also had
the feeling that it must really be nice to be a woman undergoing
intercourse. If we establish a continuity of content between these
dreams and this fantasy, which Schreber relates in close succession,
we may come to the conclusion that the memory of the illness also
awakened a memory of the doctor, and the feminine attitude of the
fantasy related from the start to the doctor. Or perhaps the dream
that the illness had returned expressed a yearning to the effect: I
wish I could see Flechsig once more. Our lack of knowledge as to
the psychic content of the first illness prevents us from getting
further with this. Perhaps a tender affection for the doctor was left
over from this condition, which, for reasons unknown to us, was
now heightened to the form of an erotic inclination. A dismayed
repudiation of the feminine fantasy, which was still kept on an
impersonal level, followed immediately, a real 'masculine protest',
to use Alfred Adler's expression, though not in the sense that he
would.[8] In the severe psychosis that is now to break out, however,
the feminine fantasy continually imposed itself, and we need to
correct the paranoid uncertainty of Schreber's way of expressing
himself only slightly in order to guess that the patient feared sexual
abuse on the part of none other than the doctor. A surge of homosexual libido was, then, the cause of this illness, its object probably
from the start Dr Flechsig, and the struggle against this libidinal
arousal produced the conflict from which the manifestations of the
illness sprang.

Let me pause for a moment in the face of a flood of remonstration
and objection. Anybody acquainted with the psychiatry of today has
to be ready for the worst.

Is it not an irresponsible slight, an indiscretion, and an act of
calumny to accuse an ethically so elevated man as the retired Presiding Judge Schreber of homosexuality? No, the patient publicly
announced his fantasy of being transformed into a woman and
overcame his personal feelings in the interests of higher insight. He
has therefore himself given us the right to concern ourselves with

this fantasy, and our translation of it into the technical terminology of medicine has not added the slightest thing to its content. – Yes, but he did that when sick: his delusion of being transformed into a woman was a pathological idea. – We have not forgotten that. We are concerned precisely with the meaning and the origin of this pathological idea. We take our cue from his own distinction between Flechsig the man and the 'Flechsig-soul'. We are not accusing him of anything, either of having homosexual impulses or of seeking to repress them. Psychiatrists should finally learn a lesson from this patient and how in spite of all his delusion he makes the effort not to confuse the world of the unconscious with the world of reality.

But surely at no point is it expressly said that the feared transformation into a woman was to be of benefit to Flechsig? – This is true, and it is not difficult to understand that in the *Memoirs*, which are intended for publication and did not wish to offend 'Flechsig' the man, such a drastic accusation is avoided. The tempering of expression that is prompted by this consideration does not however go so far as to conceal the real sense of the accusation. In fact, it can be claimed that it is indeed expressly said, for instance in the following passage: 'In this way a plot was hatched against me (around March or April 1894), which, following the recognition, or the assumption, that my nervous illness was incurable, aimed to *hand me over to a certain person in such a way* as to relinquish my soul to him, but to have my body . . . transformed into a female body and, *as such, abandoned to the person in question* for the purpose of sexual abuse . . .' (p. 56).[9] It is superfluous to remark that no other individual who might take the place of Flechsig is ever named. At the end of the stay in the Leipzig clinic the fear arises that he 'is to be thrown to the orderlies' for the purpose of sexual abuse (p. 98). The feminine attitude towards God, which is frankly admitted as the delusion develops further, removes any doubt about the role originally assigned to the doctor. The other charge raised against Flechsig echoes all too loud and clear through the book: that he sought to commit soul-murder upon him. We already know that the patient was not himself sure about the nature of this crime, but that it relates to matters of discretion which must be excluded from publication (Chapter III). A single thread offers further guidance. The soul-murder is elucidated by reference to the legendary material of Goethe's *Faust*, Lord Byron's *Manfred*, Weber's *Freischütz*, etc. (p. 22), and one of these examples is also given emphasis at another point. In the discussion of the splitting of God into two people, the 'lower' and the 'upper' God are identified by Schreber as Ahriman and Ormazd, and a little further on comes the casual remark: 'The name Ahriman, incidentally, also arises, for example, in connection with a soul-murder in Lord Byron's *Manfred*' (p. 20). In the work that is given such attention there is hardly anything which can be compared to the pact over the soul in *Faust*, and I could also find in it no trace of the term 'soul-murder', but the core and the secret of the work is – incest between siblings. Here the thread is broken short.[10]

As we intend to return to further objections in the course of this study, we now feel justified in establishing an outburst of homosexual impulses as the basis of Schreber's illness. This assumption is consonant with a notable and otherwise obscure detail of the case history. A further 'nervous collapse', which had a decisive influence on the course of his illness, befell the patient while his wife was taking a short holiday for her own recuperation. She had until then spent several hours each day with him and had joined him for lunch. When she returned after an absence of four days she found him changed in the saddest of fashions, to the extent that he now no longer wished to see her. 'The particularly decisive factor in my mental collapse was one night in which I experienced a quite unusual number of emissions (quite half a dozen) all in the single night' (p. 44). We take it to be the case that the influence of his wife's very presence protected him from the attraction of the men around him, and if we are prepared to admit that an emission can occur in an adult only where there is some psychic participation, we can supplement those nocturnal emissions with homosexual fantasies that remained unconscious.

Why this outburst of homosexual libido struck the patient precisely at that time when he found himself between his appointment and the move, we are not able to suppose without more exact knowledge of his life-story. In general human beings vacillate between heterosexual and homosexual feelings throughout their lives, and failure or disappointment on the one side tends to push them towards the other. We know of no such instances as far as Schreber is concerned; but we do not hesitate to draw attention to a somatic factor that may indeed be of relevance. At the time of this illness Dr Schreber was 51 years old and found himself at a time of life which is sexually of critical importance, a time in which the previous intensification of the sexual function in women is subject to a radical regression, the significance of which appears also to extend to men. Men, too, have a 'climacteric', with the consequent susceptibilities to illness.[11]

I can imagine how unpalatable the supposition must seem that a man's feeling of affection for a doctor can suddenly break out with new intensity eight years later,[12] and that it can serve as the cause of such a severe mental disturbance. I believe, though, that we have no right on the basis of an improbability in its internal logic to dispose of a supposition such as this, which recommends itself to us, rather than seeking to assess how far it might be taken. This improbability may be of a provisional nature, deriving from the fact that the questionable supposition is not yet fitted into context, being the first thing we have assumed in approaching the problem. For those who are unable to reserve their judgement, finding our supposition quite insupportable, we can suggest a possibility that might help it to lose its untoward character. The feeling of affection for the doctor may well spring from a 'process of transference', according to which a patient's emotional investment is removed from a person of importance for him on to the intrinsically indifferent person of the doctor, so that the doctor is selected as a substitute, a surrogate, for somebody much closer to the patient. To put it more concretely, the patient is reminded by the doctor of how his brother or his father was, he rediscovers his brother or father in him, so that in certain circumstances there can no longer be anything untoward about the yearning for this substitute person reasserting itself in him and with an intensity such as can be understood only by virtue of its roots and original significance.

In the interests of this attempt at explanation it was bound to concern me whether the patient's father was still alive at the time of his illness, or whether he had had a brother and whether any such brother was alive at that time or among the 'blissful'. I felt some satisfaction then when, after protracted searching in the *Memoirs*, I finally came upon a passage in which the patient resolves this uncertainty with the words: 'The memory of my father and my brother . . . is as sacred to me as', etc. (p. 442). Both then were already deceased at the time of the second illness (perhaps indeed of the first).

We should not, I think, object any further to the supposition that the cause of the illness was the emergence of a feminine (passively homosexual) wishful fantasy, which had taken the person of the doctor as its object. This provoked an intensive resistance on the part of Schreber's personality, and the defensive struggle, which might perhaps as easily have been pursued in other forms, elected for reasons unknown to us that of a delusion of persecution. He who had been longed for thus became a persecutor, the content of the wishful fantasy became the content of the persecution. Our conjecture is that this schematic understanding will also prove practicable for other cases of persecutory delusion. What sets the case of Schreber apart from others, however, is how it develops and the transformation that it undergoes in the course of that development.

One aspect of the transformation consists in the replacement of Flechsig by the more elevated person of God; this at first appears to signify a more acute form of conflict, an intensification of the unbearable persecution, but it soon emerges that it is preparing the way for the second transformation and so for the resolution of the conflict. If it was an impossible matter to come to terms with the role of the female prostitute in relation to the doctor, then the task of offering to God Himself the voluptuous pleasure He seeks does not encounter the same resistance on the part of the ego. Emasculation is no longer a disgrace but comes to 'accord with the World Order', entering into a grand cosmic scheme of things, and serving the purpose of a renewed creation of the human world after its demise. 'New Humans born of the Schreber spirit' will honour as their ancestor this man who thought himself the object of persecution. A way out is thereby found that satisfies both sides in the conflict. The ego is recompensed by the megalomania, while the wishful fantasy of femininity has made its way through, become acceptable. The struggle and the illness can cease. The only thing is that the thus strengthened sense of the claims of reality makes him postpone the solution from the present to some distant future, making do, so to speak, with an asymptotic wish-fulfilment.[13] The transformation into a woman is anticipated to occur at a certain point; until such a time the person of Dr Schreber will remain indestructible.

In the psychiatric textbooks we often hear of the development of megalomania out of persecutory delusion, according to the following pattern: the patient, who is primarily overtaken by the delusion that he is the object of persecution by the most powerful of forces, feels the need to find some explanation for this persecution and so comes to suppose that, as worthy of such persecution, he himself must be a lofty personage. The triggering of the megalomania is thus ascribed to a process that, following the useful formulation of E. Jones, we can call 'rationalization'. We consider it psychologically quite untenable, however, to proceed to credit rationalization with such powerfully affective consequences, and so wish to distinguish our view very clearly from that cited from the textbooks. We would not for the time being claim to know the source of megalomania.

Returning now to the Schreber Case, we have to admit that the attempt to cast light on the transformation in his delusion causes quite extraordinary difficulties. What is the path and what the means of Flechsig's elevation into God? From whence does he draw the megalomania that so happily allows a reconciliation with his persecution, and, in psychoanalytic terms, permits the assumption of the wishful fantasy that calls for repression? The *Memoirs* offer us an initial point of access here, by showing us that, for the patient, 'Flechsig' and 'God' belong to the same series. One of his fantasies allows him to eavesdrop on a conversation between Flechsig and his wife, in which the doctor introduces himself as 'God Flechsig' and is accordingly taken by her to be mad (p. 82). The following trait of the formation of Schreber's delusion also demands our attention.

Just as, when we view the whole of the delusion, the persecutor becomes divided into Flechsig and God, so Flechsig himself later splits into two personalities, the 'upper' and the 'middle' Flechsig, and God into the 'lower' and the 'upper' God. With respect to Flechsig, the splitting goes still further in the latter stages of the illness (p. 193). Such splitting is absolutely characteristic of paranoia. As hysteria condenses, so paranoia splits. Or rather, paranoia causes the condensations and identifications that have been undertaken in the unconscious fantasy to devolve once more. That this splitting repeats itself more than once in Schreber's case is, according to C. G. Jung,[14] an expression of the importance of the person in question. All of these divisions of Flechsig and God into several different persons thus have the same significance as the splitting of the persecutor into Flechsig and God. These are duplications of the same notable relationship, much as O. Rank (1909) has identified in the formation of myths. In order to interpret all of these detailed features, however, we must also draw attention to the splitting of the persecutor into Flechsig and God and the conception of this splitting as a paranoid reaction to a previously established identification between the two or to their belonging to the same series. If the persecutor Flechsig was once a loved one, then God is also nothing but the return of another similarly loved but probably more notable person.

If we proceed further with this apparently justified chain of thought, then we have to tell ourselves that this other person can be none other than the father, pushing Flechsig even more clearly into the role of the brother (who, we hope, was older).[15] The root of that feminine fantasy which set loose such resistance in the patient would thus be the erotically intensified yearning for father and brother, in the latter case passing by transference on to his doctor, Flechsig, with a settlement of the conflict being achieved through its relaying back on to the former.

If the introduction of the father into the Schreber delusion is to seem justified to us, then it must be of use for our understanding, helping to enlighten us on incomprehensible details of the delusion. We of course recall what peculiar features we found attached to

Schreber's God and to Schreber's relationship to his God. It was the most curious mix of blasphemous criticism and rebellious resistance on the one hand, with reverential devotion on the other. God, who succumbed to Flechsig's seductive influence, was not able to learn a lesson from experience, He had no knowledge of living humans because He knew only how to deal with corpses, and He expressed His power in a series of miracles, which appeared striking enough, but were ultimately insipid and silly.

The father of Justice Dr Schreber was in fact a man not without consequence. He was Dr Daniel Gottlob Moritz Schreber, whose memory is still preserved by the Schreber Associations, especially numerous in Saxony, a physician, no less, whose efforts to ensure the harmonious education of the young, the co-operation in this of family- and school-life, and the application of the care of the body and physical work to raising standards of health, were of lasting influence on his contemporaries.[16] The many editions of his *Ärztliche Zimmergymnastik* [*Medical Home Gymnastics*] to be found among our circles bear witness to his reputation as the founder of therapeutic gymnastics in Germany. Such a father was certainly not unpredisposed to be transfigured into a God in the tender memory of his son who was robbed of him so early by death. For our way of thinking there seems to exist an unbridgeable chasm between the personality of God and that of even the most illustrious human being. But we should remember that this has not always been the case. The ancient peoples were on a much closer, human footing with their gods. The dead Emperor was nothing short of deified by the Romans. When he was first taken ill, the sober and conscientious Vespasian was heard to say: 'Woe is me, methinks I am becoming a god.'[17]

The boy's infantile attitude towards his father is perfectly familiar to us; it contains the same combination of reverential subordination and rebellious resistance that we found in Schreber's relationship to his God and so acts as the unmistakable, faithfully replicated model for the latter. The fact that Schreber's father was a physician, indeed a highly regarded physician doubtless admired by his patients, explains for us the most striking character traits of his God that Schreber critically pinpoints. Can there be any stronger expression of scorn for such a physician than asserting that he understands nothing of living people and knows only how to deal with corpses? It is doubtless part of the nature of God that He performs miracles, but a physician too performs miracles, as reported by his enthusiastic clients: he carries out miracle cures. If then precisely these miracles, their material having been supplied by the patient's hypochondria, turn out to be so hard to believe, so absurd and in part silly, then we are reminded of the assertion in the *Interpretation of Dreams* that absurdity in dreams is an expression of mockery and derision.[18] Thus it serves the same representational function in paranoia. As far as other criticisms are concerned, for example that God learns nothing from experience, the probable conclusion is that we are dealing with the mechanism of the infantile 'return coach' or *tu quoque:*[19] when the criticism has been received it is directed unchanged back to where it came from, just as the voices mentioned previously (p. 23) lead us to suppose that the charge of 'soul-murder' laid against Flechsig was originally a self-accusation.[20]

Emboldened by the usefulness of the father's profession in clarifying the particular characteristics of Schreber's God, we may now venture, by means of an interpretation, to elucidate the curious structuring of the divine Being. As we know, the world of God consists of the 'frontal domains of God', also known as 'forecourts of Heaven', and containing the souls of dead humans, and of the 'lower' and the 'upper' God, who together are called 'rear domains of God' (p. 19). If we have come to terms with the fact that we cannot unfold the condensation which is present here, we can none the less use the indication we gained earlier that the 'miracled' birds, unmasked as girls, are derived from the forecourts of Heaven, in order to adopt the *frontal* domains of God and *forecourts* of Heaven as symbolic of femininity and the *rear* realms of God as symbolic of masculinity. If we could be sure that Schreber's dead brother was older than he, we could view the division of God into the lower and the upper God as the expression of the memory that after the early death of the father the elder brother took the father's place.

Finally, in this connection, I will consider the *sun*, which by virtue of its 'rays' has attained such great importance for the expression of

41

the delusion. Schreber has a quite special relationship to the sun. It speaks to him in human words and so reveals itself to him as an animate being or as the organ of a higher being that is for now hidden behind it (p. 9). From a doctor's report we learn that he 'nothing short of bellows threats and curses at it' (p. 382),[21] crying out to it that it should crawl away and be gone from his sight. He himself tells of how the sun turns pale before him.[22] The part it has in his destiny is announced by the fact that it shows important changes in appearance as soon as alterations are underway in him, as for instance in the first weeks of his stay at Sonnenstein (p. 135). Schreber helps us out with the interpretation of this solar myth. He directly identifies the sun with God, one minute with the lower God (Ahriman),[23] the next with the upper: 'On the following day . . . I saw the upper God (Ormazd), this time not with my mind's eye but with the eyes in my head. It was indeed the sun, but not the sun in its customary appearance as it is familiar to all and sundry, but', etc. (pp. 137–8). It is thus only logical if he treats it just the same as he does God Himself.

I cannot be held responsible for the monotony of the solutions provided by psychoanalysis if I assert that the sun, in its turn, is nothing other than a sublimated symbol of the father. The symbolism here disregards the grammatical gender, in German at least, for in most other languages the sun is a masculine noun. Its counterpart in this mirroring of the parental couple is what is generally referred to as 'Mother Earth'. In the psychoanalytic resolution of pathogenic fantasies in neurotics we often enough find confirmation of this proposition. I will merely cite this one example of the correlation with cosmic myths. One of my patients, who had lost his father at an early age and sought to find him once more in all that is great and sublime in nature, made me think it probable that Nietzsche's hymn 'Before Sunrise' gives expression to the same longing.[24] Another, who in his neurosis after the death of his father was subject to his first attack of anxiety and dizziness when the sun shone on him as he was working in the garden with his spade, came of his own accord to the interpretation that he had become anxious because his father had been watching him while he set about his mother with a sharp instrument. When I ventured a sober intervention, he made his view more plausible by informing me that he had already compared his father to the sun while he was still alive, albeit at that time with parodic intent. Whenever he had been asked where his father was going for the summer he answered in the resonant words of the 'Prologue in Heaven' [from *Faust I*]:

> *Und seine vorgeschriebne Reise*
> *Vollendet er mit Donnergang.*

[And his prescribèd journey he finishes with thunder-tread.]

Every year his father would follow medical advice and visit the spa resort of Marienbad. In this patient the infantile disposition towards his father had taken hold in two phases. As long as the father was alive, it took the form of total resistance and open combat, immediately after his death, a neurosis that was based upon slavish submission and retroactive obedience towards his father.

In the case of Schreber, then, we once more find ourselves on the distinctly familiar ground of the father complex.[25] If the struggle with Flechsig reveals itself to the patient as a conflict with God, we must translate the same into an infantile conflict with his beloved father, the elements of which, unknown to us, have determined the content of the delusion. None of the material that is usually uncovered by analysis in such cases is absent here; everything is represented by some hint or other. In these childhood experiences the father appears to disrupt the generally auto-erotic satisfaction that the child seeks and that is often later replaced in fantasies by a less ignoble kind.[26] In the final stage of Schreber's delusion the infantile sexual urge can celebrate a famous triumph: voluptuousness becomes God-fearing, and God Himself (the father) ceaselessly asks it of the patient. The father's most dread threat, that of castration, has furnished the material for the wishful fantasy (initially resisted and then accepted) of being transformed into a woman. The allusion to an offence, which is covered by the surrogate formation 'soul-murder', is more than clear. His chief orderly is found to be identical with his housemate, von W., who, according to the voices, falsely accused him of masturbation (p. 108). The voices say, as though in justification for the threat of castration: 'Because you are said to be *represented* as in thrall to voluptuous excesses' (pp. 127–8).[27] Finally, the compulsion to think (p. 47), to which the patient submits because he assumes that, if he stops thinking for a moment, God will believe him to have become stupid and so withdraw from him, is the reaction, familiar to us from elsewhere, against the threat or the fear that sexual activity, specifically masturbation, will lead to the loss of reason.[28] Given the extraordinary number of hypochondriac delusional ideas that the patient develops,[29] we should probably not attribute too great an importance to the fact that some of the same coincide word for word with the hypochondriac fears of masturbators.[30]

For anybody prepared to be bolder than I or who, through connections to the Schreber family, might know more of the people concerned, of the milieu, and of minor occurrences, it would be an easy task to trace countless details of Schreber's delusion back to their sources and so to recognize their significance, this in spite of the censorship to which the *Memoirs* are subjected. We have no choice but to be content with this shadowy sketch of the infantile material, through which the paranoid condition has represented the current conflict.

I might add a further word on the cause of that conflict which broke out with regard to the feminine wishful fantasy. We know that our task is to make a connection between the appearance of a wishful fantasy and a *frustration*, a deprivation in real life. Schreber indeed admits to such a deprivation. His marriage, pictured as happy in other respects, was not blessed for him with children, above all with the son who might have given him solace for the loss of his father and brother, and so acted as a channel for the unsatisfied homosexual affection.[31] His family line was threatened with extinction, and it seems that he had some pride in his birth and lineage. 'For the Flechsigs and the Schrebers both belonged to what is known as "the highest heavenly nobility"; the Schrebers in particular bore the title "Margraves of Tuscany and Tasmania" in accordance with the custom among the souls of being led by their personal vanity into decorating themselves with rather highfalutin worldly titles' (p. 24).[32] The great Napoleon divorced his Josephine, though not without having gone through severe inner struggles, because she was unable to continue his dynasty.[33] Dr Schreber appears to have formed the fantasy that if he were a woman he would be more successful in having children and so to have found a way back to the feminine attitude towards his father of his early childhood years. The delusion, which would later be postponed ever further into the future, that the world would come to be populated through his emasculation with 'New Humans born of the Schreber spirit' (p. 288) was thus also designed to alleviate his childlessness. If the 'little men' that Schreber himself finds so mysterious are children, then we can well understand how they come to congregate in great numbers upon his head (p. 158); they are indeed the 'children of his spirit'. (Cf. my remark on the representation of descent from the father and on the birth of Athene in the case history of the Rat Man.)

Notes

1. C. G. Jung [*Über die Psychologie der Dementia praecox*] (1907).

2. Dr Weber's Assessment states: 'If one considers the content of his writings, the many indiscretions in relation to himself and others, the frank portrayal of the most dubious and aesthetically quite impossible situations and processes, the use of the most offensive kinds of strong language, etc., then one will fail to understand how a man who otherwise stood out for his tact and finer feeling could intend a course of action that would so severely compromise him in the public eye, unless, that is . . .', etc. (p. 402). One can hardly expect a case history which has to depict human nature in distress and its struggle for reassertion to be 'discreet' and 'aesthetically' satisfying.

3. From the Preface (p. viii): 'Even now your name is called to me hundreds of times every day by the voices that speak with me, in constantly recurrent connections, in particular as the originator of those injuries, even though the personal relations that existed between us have long receded for me into the background, so that in myself I would hardly have any cause to be reminded of you again and again, still less with any sense of resentment.'

4. According to another significant but soon-to-be-rejected version, Prof. Flechsig had shot himself, either at Weißenburg in Alsace or in police imprisonment in Leipzig. The patient saw his funeral procession, but this did not take the direction towards the cemetery that one would expect, given the position of the university clinic. At other times Flechsig appeared to him in the company of a policeman or in conversation with his wife, which he witnessed by way of a nerve-connection, with Prof. Flechsig calling himself 'God Flechsig' to his wife, who was thus inclined to think him insane (p. 82).

5. The voices told him that in an inquest this von W. had, either with intent or through carelessness, claimed false things about him, not least that he was guilty of masturbation; his punishment was now to have to wait on the patient (p. 108).

6. 'I must thus *recognize the possibility* that everything reported in the first sections of my *Memoirs* about events connected with the name Flechsig, is not to be related to the living person but to Flechsig the soul, which is not to be confused with that person and the independent existence of which is beyond dispute, though not to be explained in natural terms' (pp. 342–3).

7. See K. Abraham ['Die psychosexuellen Differenzen der Hysterie und der Dementia praecox', *Zentbl. Nervenheilk.* 19] (1908). In this work the conscientious author acknowledges the influence derived from our correspondence on the development of his views.

8. [A.] Adler ['Der psychische Hermaphroditismus im Leben und in der Neurose', *Fortschr. Med.* 28] (1910). – According to Adler the masculine protest participates in the production of the symptom, while in the present case the individual is protesting against the completed symptom.

9. The emphasis is mine.

10. To reinforce the assertion above: Manfred tells the demon who would fetch him out of life (final scene):

> . . . my past power
> was purchased by no compact with thy crew.

A pact over the soul is thus directly contradicted. This error of Schreber's is probably not innocent. – It was plausible, incidentally, for the content of *Manfred* to be connected to the repeatedly asserted incestuous relationship between the poet and his half-sister, and it is certainly striking that Byron's other drama, the magnificent *Cain*, plays among the primal family in which incest between siblings could raise no objection. – Neither should we leave the theme of soul-murder without also recalling the following passage: 'while at an earlier stage Flechsig was named as the originator of the soul-murder, for quite a time now I myself have been "represented" as the one who is supposed to have committed soul-murder, by an intentional twisting of our relationship . . .' (p. 23).

11. I owe this knowledge of Schreber's age at the time of his illness to helpful information on the part of his relatives, collected for me by Dr Stegmann in Dresden. Otherwise this study confines itself entirely to material to be found in the *Memoirs* themselves.

12. The interval between Schreber's first and second bouts of illness.

13. Towards the end of the book we read: 'Only in terms of possibilities that might arise here, I would mention the emasculation that has yet to be executed, with the effect that by means of divine fertilization a new generation would issue from my womb.'

14. C. G. Jung ['Ein Beitrag zur Psychologie des Gerüchtes', *Zentbl. Psychoanal.* I] (1910). Jung is probably right when he goes on to argue that, in line with the general tendency of schizophrenia, this splitting works analytically, causing a breakdown in potency aimed at preventing the development of impressions of an unacceptable strength. The words of one of his women patients: 'Oh, are you another Dr J.? Somebody claiming to be Dr J. already came to see me this morning,' should however be translated as an admission: 'You now remind me of a different instance from my series of transferences to that of your last visit.'

15. The *Memoirs* offer no enlightenment here.

16. My colleague Dr Stegmann in Dresden was good enough to send for my perusal an edition of a magazine entitled *Der Freund der Schreber-Vereine* [*The Friend of the Schreber Associations*]. In this number (Year 2, no. 10) biographical details of the life of the celebrated Dr Schreber are provided to mark the hundredth anniversary of his birth. Dr Schreber senior was born in 1808 and died in 1861 at the age of only 53. From the source cited earlier I know that our patient was 19 years old at that time.

17. See Suetonius, *Lives of the Caesars*, Chapter 23. This deification originated with Julius Caesar. Augustus styled himself '*Divi filius*' in his inscriptions.

18. *Interpretation of Dreams* (1900) [VI.G].

19. Absolutely typical of such revenge is when the patient one day notes down the sentence: '*Any attempt at achieving an external educational influence must be abandoned as hopeless*' (p. 188). It is God who is uneducable.

20. 'For quite a time now I myself have been "represented" as the one who is supposed to have committed soul-murder, by an intentional twisting of our relationship,' etc.

21. 'The sun is a whore' (p. 384).

22. 'The sun at any rate has a quite different image for me now than in the time before my illness. Its rays pale before me when I address it loudly. I can calmly look into the sun and am dazzled only to a very modest extent, whereas in my healthy days I could no more have looked into the sun for a full minute than I suppose anybody else could' (p. 139 n.).

23. 'Now (since July 1894) He is directly identified with the sun by the voices which speak to me' (p. 88).

24. From *Thus Spake Zarathustra*, Part Three. – Nietzsche too had known his father only as a child.

25. Just as the 'feminine wishful fantasy' is but one of the typical forms of the infantile nuclear complex.

26. See the remarks on the analysis of the 'Rat Man' (1909).

27. The systems of 'representation and writing up' (pp. 126–7) suggest, in connection with the 'tested souls', experiences at school.

28. 'That this was the goal to be pursued was earlier admitted to me in the phrase issuing from the upper God which I heard innumerable times: "We want to destroy your reason"' (p. 206 n.).

29. I must point out here that I will consider a theory of paranoia trustworthy only when it has managed coherently to account for the *hypochondriac* symptoms that more or less regularly accompany it. I believe that hypochondria has the same status for paranoia as does anxiety neurosis for hysteria.

30. 'They thus tried to pump out my spinal cord, using so-called "little men" who were set into my feet. I will have more to say about these "little men" who showed some relation to the phenomenon of the same name already discussed in Chapter VI; in general there were two of them in each case, a "little Flechsig" and a "little von W.", whose voices I could also hear in my feet' (p. 154) – Von W. is the same one who was responsible for the charge of masturbation. Schreber himself describes the 'little men' as one of the most notable and, in a certain connection, most mysterious of phenomena (p. 157). It seems that they sprang from a condensation of children and – spermatozoa.

31. 'After I recovered from my first illness I spent eight on the whole very happy years with my wife, years rich in public honours and only dimmed from time to time by the recurrent dashing of our hopes that the marriage might be blessed with children' (p. 36).

32. Following on from this remark, where the wry good nature of healthier days is preserved in spite of the delusion, he pursues the relations between the Flechsig and the Schreber families into previous centuries in the style of a young man who cannot comprehend how he could live for so many long years without any knowledge of his beloved fiancée and is convinced that they were acquainted with each other in earlier times.

33. In this connection it is worth mentioning the patient's protestation against a statement in the medical report: 'I have never entertained the idea of a *divorce* or shown any sort of indifference with regard to the continuance of the bonds of marriage, contrary to the impression one might have from the terms used in the report that "I am always quick to retort that my wife can seek a divorce then"' (p. 436).

III

On the Paranoid Mechanism

Thus far we have dealt with the father complex, which dominates Schreber's case, and the central wishful fantasy of the illness. In all of this there is nothing which is characteristic of the form of illness that is paranoia, nothing which we might not encounter, and indeed have, in other cases of neurosis. We must locate the peculiar character of paranoia (or of paranoid dementia) elsewhere, in the particular manifestation of the symptoms, and these we would expect to ascribe not to the complexes but to the mechanism of symptom formation or that of repression. We would say that the paranoid character lies in the fact that the reaction used to fend off a homosexual wishful fantasy is precisely a persecution delusion of this kind.

This is all the more significant if we heed the voice of experience and attribute to the homosexual wishful fantasy in particular a more intimate, perhaps constant, relationship to the form of illness in question. Inclined to mistrust my own experience in this matter, over the last few years I have joined with my friends C. G. Jung in Zurich and S. Ferenczi in Budapest to examine from this point of view a series of cases of paranoid illness under their observation. Those whose case histories were examined by us were both men and women, of different races, professions and degrees of social standing, and we noted with surprise how clearly the defence against a homosexual wish was to be recognized at the core of the pathological conflict in each of these cases and how all of them had come to grief in trying to overcome their unconsciously intensified homosexuality.[1] This was not at all in line with our expectations. In paranoia, in particular, the sexual aetiology is in no sense obvious, with social humiliations and setbacks tending to be to the fore in its causation, especially in the case of men. We need only forge a little deeper, however, to recognize that the driving force in these social injuries is the part played by the homosexual components of the patient's emotional life. As long as normal activity prevents us from gaining insight into the depths of the life of the soul, we are inclined to doubt that the emotional relations between an individual and those around him in his social existence have anything to do with eroticism, in their factual character or their genesis. Delusions regularly serve to uncover these relations and trace the social emotion back to its root in the blatant sensuality of the erotic wish. Dr Schreber too, whose delusion culminates unmistakably in a homosexual wishful fantasy, had, according to all the reports, displayed no sign of homosexuality in any vulgar sense for as long as he was healthy.

I believe that it is neither superfluous nor unjustified for me to seek to show that our current comprehension of the processes of the soul, as gained through psychoanalysis, may already mediate for us an understanding of the role of the homosexual wish in the onset of paranoia. Recent investigations[2] have made us aware of a stage in the developmental history of the libido that is passed through on the way from auto-eroticism to object-love.[3] It has been called *Narzissismus* [narcissism], though I prefer the perhaps less correct but shorter and less clumsy-sounding *Narziβmus*. It consists in the individual, caught up in his development, assembling his auto-erotically active sexual drives into a unity in order to gain an object of love and first taking himself, his own body, as that object, before moving on from this to the choice of another person. A phase of this kind, mediating between auto-eroticism and the choice of an object, is perhaps in the normal course of things essential; it seems that many people are held up in it for an unusual length of time and that much is retained from it for later stages of development. The most important aspect of this self, taken as an object of love, may already be the genitals. The path leads on to the choice of an object with similar genitals, in other words via a homosexual object-choice, to heterosexuality. We assume that those who are manifest homosexuals in later life have never freed themselves from the demand for genitals similar to their own in their object, a considerable influence being derived from children's sexual theories, which at first ascribe the same genitals to both sexes.

After the attainment of the heterosexual object-choice, the homosexual inclinations are not, though, suspended or discontinued, but simply pushed away from the sexual object and diverted into new uses. They join up with portions of the ego-drives and serve as 'attached' components to help constitute the social drives, thus contributing an erotic element to friendship, camaraderie, sense of community, and to the general love of mankind. One could hardly assess the extent of these contributions from an erotic source where the sexual object is inhibited if one were to go by the normal social relations of human beings. It is, however, pertinent to note here that precisely manifest homosexuals, and among them especially those that resist physical activity, are marked out by particularly intensive participation in those general interests of humanity that have arisen through the sublimation of eroticism.

In the *Three Essays on the Theory of Sexuality* I put forward the view that each psychosexual stage of development produces the possibility of 'fixation' and thus a dispositional point. People who have not fully released themselves from the stage of narcissism, and thus have a fixation there that can lead to a pathological disposition, are open to the danger that a flood of libido which finds no other outlet may subject their social drives to sexualization and so reverse the sublimations that they have achieved in the course of their development. This result may be brought about by anything that provokes a backward flow of the libido ('regression'): on the one hand when it is collaterally reinforced by disappointment with women or directly dammed up by mishaps in social relations with men – both examples of 'frustration' – and equally, on the other hand, when it is subject to a general increase which is too powerful to be dispensed through channels already open to it and so bursts through the dam at the weak point in its structure. As our analyses reveal that paranoiacs *seek to fend off such sexualization of their investments of social drive*, we are forced to suppose that the weak point in their development is to be found in that portion between auto-eroticism, narcissism and homosexuality, that it is there that their pathological disposition (which may yet be more precisely defined) lies. We would attribute such a disposition to Kraepelin's dementia praecox or what Bleuler has called *schizophrenia*, and we would hope in what follows to gain more evidence that will enable us to find the causes of the differences in form and outcome of the two conditions by locating corresponding variations in their dispositional fixations.

If we can thus take the idea of the homosexual wishful fantasy, *to love the man*, as the core of the conflict in male paranoia, we must certainly not forget that the precondition for securing such a significant assumption would be the investigation of a large number of cases of every form of paranoid illness. We must therefore be prepared for the possibility that our claim will have to be restricted to just one type of paranoia. It is none the less striking that the principal forms of paranoia familiar to us can all be represented as contradictions of the one proposition '*I* (a man) *love him* (a man)', indeed that they exhaust all possible formulations of this contradiction.

The proposition 'I love him (the man)' is contradicted by

a) the delusion of *persecution*, which proclaims loud and clear:

'I do not *love* him – indeed, I *hate* him.' This contradiction, which could not be put in any other way in the unconscious,[4] cannot however become conscious in this form for the paranoiac. The mechanism of symptom formation in paranoia demands that feeling as inner perception should be replaced by a perception from without. Thus the proposition 'Indeed, I hate him' is transformed by *projection* into another: '*He hates* (persecutes) *me*, which will entitle me to hate him.' The driving unconscious feeling thus appears to be the consequence of an external perception:

'Indeed, I do not *love* him – I *hate* him, indeed – because *he persecutes me.*'

Observation removes any doubt that the persecutor is any other than the erstwhile beloved.

b) A further point of access for the contradiction is *erotomania*, which would remain incomprehensible from any other angle.

'I do not love *him* – indeed, it is *her* I love.'

And the same compulsion to project imposes the following trans-formation on the proposition: 'I can tell that *she* loves me.'

'I do not love *him* – indeed, it is *her* I love – because *she loves me.*' Many cases of erotomania might give the impression of exaggerated or distorted heterosexual fixations with no other reason behind them, if we were not alert to the fact that all these infatu-ations start not with the internal perception of loving but one of being loved that comes from outside. In this form of paranoia, though, the intermediate sentence 'I love *her*' can also become conscious, because its contradiction of the first sentence is not as pronounced or as untenable as that between loving and hating. It is after all possible also to love *her* alongside *him*. In this way it can occur that the projective substitution '*She loves me*' may recede in relation to the 'elementary language' proposition: 'Indeed, it is *her* I love.'

c) The third and final possible type of contradiction would be by way of a delusion of *jealousy*, which we can study in its characteristic forms in both men and women.

a) The delusion of jealousy in the alcoholic. The role of alcohol in this disorder is in every way understandable to us. We know that this source of pleasure suspends inhibitions and reverses subli-mations. Men are not infrequently driven to alcohol by their dis-appointment with women, which is to say that, as a rule, a man resorts to a public-house and to the company of men, affording him the emotional satisfaction that was lacking at home with his wife. If these men, though, become objects of a more powerful libidinal investment in his unconscious, then he fends this off by the third version of the contradiction:

'It is not *I* who love the man – indeed, it is *she who loves him*' – thus suspecting his wife with regard to all the men whom he is tempted to love.

The distortion through projection is necessarily absent here, as the change in the subject who does the loving means that the process is at any rate cast out of the self. That the woman loves the men remains a matter of external perception; that the man himself hates rather than loves, that he loves that person rather than this, these are indeed facts of internal perception.

β) Paranoid jealousy among women is produced in a quite analogous fashion.

'It is not *I* who love the women – rather *he loves them.*' The jealous woman suspects her husband with regard to all the women she herself likes as a result of the disposition caused by narcissism, which has become excessive, and of her homosexuality. In the choice of the love-objects that have been diverted on to the husband the influence of the period of life in which the fixation came about is unmistakably revealed; they are often older persons, unsuitable for real love, revivals of the carers, servants and friends of childhood or even directly of the sisters who were seen as rivals.

One might think that a proposition consisting of three parts such as '*I love him*' would admit only of three types of contradiction. The delusion of jealousy contradicts the subject, the delusion of persecution the verb, and erotomania the object. However, there is in fact a fourth possible form of contradiction, the utter rejection of the whole proposition:

'*I do not love at all, not anybody*' – and, as one has to channel one's libido somewhere, this proposition appears to be the psychological equivalent of: 'I love only myself.' This type of contradiction, then, would present us with megalomania, which we conceive of as a *sexual overestimation of one's own self* and can therefore stand side-by-side with the familiar overestimation of the object of love.[5]

The fact that an added element of megalomania can be ascertained in most other forms of paranoid illness will be of some importance for other parts of the theory of paranoia. We are entitled to suppose that megalomania is intrinsically infantile and that in later development it is sacrificed to society; it is after all suppressed by no other influence as intensively as when an individual is overpowered by infatuation.

> *Denn wo die Lieb' erwachet, stirbt*
> *das Ich, der finstere Despot.*[6]

[For where love awakes, so dies the self, the dark despot.]

Following this consideration of the unexpected significance for paranoia of the homosexual wishful fantasy we can return to those two factors to which we wanted from the outset to assign what is characteristic about this form of illness: to the mechanism of *the formation of symptoms* and to that of *repression.*

In the first instance we certainly have no justification in taking these two mechanisms to be identical or assuming that the formation of symptoms proceeds along the same course as repression, taking the same path but moving in the opposite direction. Such identity between them is at any rate hardly very likely; but let us reserve our judgement in this matter until the investigation is carried out.

In the formation of symptoms in paranoia the feature that earns the name *projection* is especially striking. An internal perception is suppressed and, by way of substitute, its content, having undergone a degree of distortion, is consciously registered as an external perception. In delusions of persecution distortion consists in a transformation of affect; that which should have been felt internally as love is perceived as hate from without. One might be tempted to deem this curious process the most significant aspect of paranoia and absolutely pathognomonic for it, were it not for the timely reminder that, first, projection does not play the same role in all forms of paranoia and, second, that it arises not only in paranoia but also in other psychic conditions, indeed that it is assigned a regular share in our attitude to the external world. If, instead of looking for the causes of certain sensations within ourselves, as we otherwise do, we locate them externally, then this normal procedure deserves to be called projection. Thus made aware that the understanding of projection involves more general psychological problems, we are resolved to save the study of projection and so of the whole mechanism of paranoid symptom-formation for a future occasion, and turn to the question as to what sorts of conception we may form of the mechanism of repression in paranoia. In justification of our provisional renunciation, let me note from the start that we will find that the process of repression is much more intimately connected in its character to the developmental history of the libido and to the disposition that it produces than is the formation of symptoms.

In psychoanalysis we have broadly seen pathological phenomena to be derived from repression. If we take a closer look at that which we call 'repression' then we have reason to divide the process into three phases, which allow for good conceptual differentiation.

1) The first phase consists in *fixation*, the forerunner and the precondition of each and every 'repression'. The fact of fixation might be described as follows: a drive, or a component of one, fails to follow the development that is anticipated as normal and remains confined to a more infantile stage on account of this developmental inhibition. The relevant libidinal flow is related to later psychic formations as would befit one that belongs to the system of the unconscious, one that is repressed. We have already said that in such fixations of drives resides the disposition towards the later development of illness and, we can add, above all the determination of the outcome of the third phase of repression.

2) The second phase of repression is the actual repression, upon which we have primarily focused hitherto. It springs from the more highly developed systems of the ego, those capable of consciousness, and can actually be described as an 'after-pressure'. It gives the impression of being a fundamentally active process, while fixation presents itself essentially as a passive retardation. It may be the psychic derivatives of those primarily retarded drives that are subject to repression, where their strengthening has led to a conflict between them and the ego (or drives according with the ego), or it may be such psychic tendencies as provoke a strong antipathy for other reasons. This antipathy would not, however, result in repression if a connection were not made between the unsympathetic tendencies that are to be repressed and those which have already undergone repression. Where this is the case, the rejection of the conscious systems and the attraction of the unconscious are concerted in effecting a successful repression. The two cases distinguished here may in reality not be so starkly separated, only differentiated by a more or less significant contribution from the primarily repressed drives.

3) The third phase to be noted here, and the most significant for the pathological phenomena, is that of the failure of the repression,

the *breakthrough*, or *return of the repressed*. This breakthrough proceeds from the point of fixation, and its content is a regression of the libidinal development to that point.

We have already mentioned the diverse varieties of fixation, of which there are as many as there are stages in the development of the libido. We must be prepared for other forms of variety in the mechanisms of actual repression and in those of the breakthrough (or the formation of symptoms) and may probably already assume that we will not be able to trace all of these varieties back to the developmental history of the libido alone.

It is not difficult to surmise that our discussion is touching here upon the problem of the choice of neurosis, which, however, may not be tackled before preparatory work of other kinds has been achieved. Remembering that we have already dealt with fixation and set the formation of symptoms aside, we will confine ourselves to the question of whether the analysis of the Schreber Case can allow us to gain a clue as to the mechanism of (actual) repression that is predominant in paranoia.

At the peak of the illness, under the influence of visions 'in part gruesome in nature, in part, though, of indescribable magnificence' (p. 73), there developed in Schreber the conviction of a great catastrophe, of the end of the world. Voices told him that the work of the 14,000 years past was now lost, that a duration of only 212 years was still in store for the world (p. 71). In the final part of his stay at Flechsig's asylum, he believed this time had already elapsed. He himself was the 'only real human still surviving', and the few human forms he still saw, the doctor, the orderlies and patients, he explained as being 'miracled up, fleetingly improvised men'. From time to time the reciprocal current broke through; a newspaper was presented to him that contained news of his own death (p. 81), he himself existed in a second, inferior shape and one day had quietly passed away in the same (p. 73). But the form of the delusions that held fast to the self and sacrificed the world proved to be much the stronger. He had various ideas about the causes of this catastrophe; first he thought of glaciation through the retraction of the sun, then of destruction by earthquake, with him as 'seer of spirits' acting as prime mover in much the same way as another seer was said to have done in the Lisbon earthquake of 1755 (p. 91). Or it was Flechsig who was culpable, having used his magic powers to spread fear and terror among mankind, to destroy the foundations of religion, and bring about a general state of nervous disorder and immorality, in the wake of which devastating pestilences had been visited upon humanity (p. 91). At any rate, the end of the world was the result of the conflict that had broken out between Flechsig and himself or, in terms of the aetiology of the second phase of the delusion, his now indissoluble bond with God, the necessary consequence, that is, of his illness. Years later, when Dr Schreber had returned to human society and could find nothing in the books, musical scores or other articles of general use now restored to him that was consistent with the postulation of a great temporal chasm in the history of humanity, he admitted that his view could no longer be maintained: '. . . I cannot help but acknowledge that *viewed externally* all has remained as it always was. *Whether a profound internal change has none the less taken place* will be discussed further on' (pp. 84–5). He had no doubt that the world had come to an end during his illness and what he now saw before him was, in spite of appearances, a different one.

A similar global catastrophe is not infrequently encountered in the tempestuous phase of paranoia in other case histories.[7] Based on our understanding of libidinal investment, and led by the evaluation of other humans as 'fleetingly improvised men', we will encounter no difficulty in explaining these catastrophes.[8] The patient has withdrawn the libidinal investment hitherto lodged with them from the people around him and from the world outside as a whole; everything has thus become indifferent and unrelated to him and has to be explained through a secondary rationalization as 'miracled up, fleetingly improvised'. The end of the world is the projection of this internal catastrophe; his subjective world has come to an end since he withdrew his love from it.[9]

After the curse with which Faust declares his freedom from the world, the chorus of spirits sings:

Weh! weh!
Du hast sie zerstört,
die schöne Welt,
mit mächtiger Faust;
Sie stürzt, sie zerfällt!
Ein Halbgott hat sie zerschlagen!
. . .
Mächtiger
der Erdensöhne,
Prächtiger
baue sie wieder,
in deinem Busen baue sie auf!

[Woe! woe! You have destroyed it, the beauteous world, with mighty fist; it falls, it breaks up! A demigod has smashed it! . . . Mighty one among the sons of the earth, more splendid build it once more, in your breast build it up!]

And the paranoiac builds it up once more, not more splendid perhaps, but at least in such a way that he can live in it again. He builds it up through the work of his delusion. *What we take to be the production of the illness, the formation of the delusion, is in reality the attempt at a cure, the reconstruction.* This succeeds more or less well after the catastrophe, but never fully; a 'profound internal change', as Schreber has it, has befallen the world. But the individual has regained a relationship to the people and things of the world, often a very intensive one, even if what was once a relationship of expectant tenderness may now be one of hostility. We would say, then, that the real process of repression consists in a detachment of the libido from once-loved persons – and things. It happens silently; we have no intelligence of it, and are forced to work by inference from the processes that follow it. What does clamour for our attention is the process of recovery that reverses the repression and leads the libido back to those whom it had abandoned. In paranoia this proceeds by way of projection. It was not correct to say that the internally suppressed perception is projected outwards; rather, we see that that which has been suspended within returns from without. The thorough investigation of the process of projection, which we have deferred to another time, will put this matter securely beyond doubt.

If our newfound insight requires us to pursue a series of further discussions, then this is no cause for dissatisfaction.

1) A first consideration tells us that a detachment of the libido is neither exclusive to paranoia nor so disastrous in its consequences when it arises elsewhere. It is quite possibly the case that the detachment of the libido is the essential and regular mechanism of every type of repression; knowledge of this must escape us until the other repressive disorders have been made subject to analogous investigation. It is certain that in the normal life of the soul (and not only in mourning) we constantly carry out such detachments of the libido from people or other objects without succumbing to illness. When Faust declares himself free of the world with his cursings, no paranoia or other kind of neurosis results from this, but a certain general psychic state. The removal of libido in itself cannot, therefore, account for what is pathogenic in paranoia; a particular characteristic is required, which can differentiate the paranoid detachment of libido from other types of the same process. Such a characteristic may easily be proposed. To what further use is the libido that has become free through detachment put? Normally we straightaway seek a substitute for the connection that has been lifted. Until this substitution has succeeded the free libido is left suspended in the psyche where it produces tensions and influences mood; in hysteria the liberated portion of libido transforms itself into bodily innervations or into anxiety. In paranoia, though, we have a clinical indication that the libido withdrawn from the object is channelled into a special kind of use. We recall that most cases of paranoia display an element of megalomania and that megalomania can in itself constitute a paranoia. From this we would conclude that in paranoia the liberated libido is diverted to the ego and used for its aggrandizement. Thus, the stage of narcissism, familiar from the development of the libido, where one's own ego is the only sexual object, has been reached once more. In view of this clinical evidence we would assume that the paranoid have brought with them a

fixation in narcissism and we can assert that the *backward step from sublimated homosexuality to narcissism* provides the element of *regression* that is characteristic of paranoia.

2) A no less plausible objection can find support in Schreber's case history (as in many others), which makes it clear that the delusion of persecution (in relation to Flechsig) unmistakably emerges earlier than the fantasy of the end of the world, so that the ostensible return of the repressed precedes the repression itself, in a manner that is patently nonsensical. To give this objection its due we must step down from the level of general observation to a detailed evaluation of the doubtless much more complicated real situation. The possibility must be conceded that such a detachment of the libido may just as well be partial, a retraction from a single complex, as general. The partial detachment, initially motivated only by influences encountered in life, is probably by far the more frequent and the one that introduces its general counterpart. The detachment may then remain partial or it may be composed into a general one that proclaims itself strikingly through megalomania. In the case of Schreber the detachment of the libido from the person of Flechsig was probably indeed the primary instance; it is immediately followed by the delusion that leads the libido back to Flechsig (under a negative sign to show that repression has taken place) and so abolishes the work of repression. Now the struggle for repression breaks out anew, this time, however, availing itself of more powerful means; in as far as the contested object becomes the most important one in the external world, on the one hand wanting to draw all libido to itself and on the other mobilizing all forms of resistance against itself, the struggle for the single object becomes comparable to a general battle, in the course of which the victory of repression is expressed by the conviction that the world has ended and only the self has survived. If one reviews the artful constructions that Schreber's delusion erects on religious ground (the hierarchy of God – the souls in ordeal – the forecourts of Heaven – the lower and the upper God), then one can gauge in retrospect what a wealth of sublimations was caused to collapse by the catastrophe of the general detachment of the libido.

3) A third consideration, which presents itself on the basis of the views developed here, prompts the question as to whether we should take the general detachment of the libido from the external world to be effective enough to provide an explanation for the 'end of the world', or whether in this case the ego-investments that were retained would not have been sufficient to preserve the rapport with the outside world. We would then either have to deem what we call libidinal investment (interest with erotic sources) identical with interest in general or consider the possibility that a substantial disturbance in the accommodation of the libido can also induce a corresponding disturbance in the ego-investments. These are problems that leave us feeling clumsy and helpless in our search for an answer. If we could work on the basis of a secure theory of the drives, it would be otherwise; but the truth is that we have nothing of the sort. We locate the drive on the conceptual border where the somatic meets the realm of the psyche, regarding it as the psychic representative of organic powers, and adopt the popular distinction between ego-drives and the sexual drive, which seems to us to concur with the biological dualism of individual creatures that strive both for their own preservation and for that of the species. Beyond this, though, we have only constructions that we erect and then readily abandon again in order to orient ourselves in the confusion of the darker psychic processes, and we expect psychoanalytic investigations of pathological psychic processes in particular to impose upon us certain decisions in questions of the theory of the drives. Given the young years and the isolated state of such investigations, this expectation cannot yet have been realized. It is no more permissible to reject out of hand the possibility of disturbances of the libido having a reactive effect on the ego-investments than the converse: the secondary or induced disturbance of libidinal processes by abnormal changes in the ego. Indeed, it is probable that processes of this kind account for the distinctive character of psychosis. How much of this may apply to paranoia cannot at present be said. Let me simply draw out a single aspect. It cannot be claimed that the paranoiac has fully withdrawn his interest from the external world, even at the height of repression, as one is compelled to say of

other forms of hallucinatory psychosis (viz. Meynert's amentia). He perceives the outside world, he takes account of changes in it, is prompted by its impressions to establish explanations (the 'fleetingly improvised' men), and so I consider it much more likely that his altered relation to the world is to be explained entirely or principally by the loss of his libidinal interest.

4) In view of the close relations between paranoia and dementia praecox one is bound to ask what sort of implications such a conception of the first disorder must have for the second. I consider that Kraepelin's step of merging what was once known as paranoia with catatonia and other forms as a new clinical entity was entirely justified, even if the name dementia praecox is an anything but apposite one to choose for it. In the case of Bleuler's designation of schizophrenia for the same group of forms, we might also object that the name appears only to be really useful if one forgets its literal meaning. It otherwise tends to be all too prejudicial, deriving a name from one theoretically postulated characteristic, and one at that which does not apply exclusively to the disorder in question and, in the light of other considerations, cannot be deemed to be the essential one. On the whole, though, the names we give to the clinical pictures are not of great importance. It would seem more essential to me to hold on to the status of paranoia as an autonomous clinical type, even if the picture it presents is so frequently complicated by schizophrenic features. For, from the point of view of the theory of the libido, while it shares with dementia praecox the principal characteristic of the repression proper – the detachment of the libido and resultant regression to the ego – it can be distinguished from it through a different location in its dispositional fixation and a different mechanism for the return of the repressed (the formation of symptoms). I would consider it most appropriate to give dementia praecox the name *paraphrenia*, which, having no determinate content in itself, expresses the disorder's relations to the securely named paranoia and at the same time recalls the hebephrenia that has been subsumed by it. It is of no concern that this name has already been proposed for a different purpose as these other usages have failed to establish themselves.

Abraham (loc. cit.) has argued most trenchantly that in dementia praecox the retraction of the libido from the external world is of a particularly pronounced character. From this characteristic we infer repression as a result of the detachment of the libido. We also regard the phase of tempestuous hallucinations as one of struggle between repression and an attempt at recovery, which seeks to restore the libido to its objects. With extraordinary analytic acuity, Jung has recognized in the deleria and motor stereotypies of the illness the vestiges of earlier object-investments, which are rigidly clung to. This attempt at cure, which the observer takes to be the illness itself, does not however make use of projection like paranoia, but rather of the hallucinatory (hysterical) mechanism. This is one of the two considerable ways in which it differs from paranoia; it may also be explained genetically from another direction. The outcome of dementia praecox, in those cases where the disorder does not remain too partial, accounts for the second difference. In general this outcome is less favourable than in paranoia; victory here belongs not, as in the latter, to reconstruction, but to repression. The regression does not merely extend to narcissism, as expressed through megalomania, but to a complete abandonment of object-love and a return to infantile auto-eroticism. The dispositional fixation must therefore lie further back than that of paranoia, contained in the beginnings of the development that strives away from auto-eroticism and towards object-love. It is also in no way probable that the homosexual impulses that we so often, even regularly, find in paranoia play a similarly significant part in the aetiology of the much less restricted disorder of dementia praecox.

Our assumptions as to the dispositional fixations in paranoia and paraphrenia would make it quite understandable that a case can begin with paranoid symptoms and yet develop into dementia, that paranoid and schizophrenic phenomena may combine in any proportion, and that a clinical picture such as Schreber's can arise, deserving the name of paranoid dementia, one which in the emergence of the wishful fantasy and hallucinations shows itself beholden to the paraphrenic character of the disorder, and in its root cause, its mechanism of projection, and its outcome, beholden to the paranoid character. Several fixations may well have been left behind in the course of the development, allowing each in their turn for the breakthrough of the evicted libido, beginning, perhaps, with one that was acquired later and, in the further course of the illness, moving on to the original one, which lies closer to the point of departure. We should like to know what conditions are responsible for the relatively favourable dispensation in the present case, given that one would be disinclined to attribute the outcome entirely to something as arbitrary as the 'improvement on transfer' that came about after the patient's departure from Flechsig's asylum.[10] But our insufficient knowledge of the intimate connections within this case history makes any answer to this interesting question impossible. One might conjecture that the reconciliation with the homosexual fantasy and so something approaching a recovery was enabled by the essentially positive tone of the father complex and a relationship in reality to his excellent father, which, during later years, was most likely undimmed.

As I neither fear criticism nor shy away from self-criticism, I have no motive for avoiding mention of a similarity that may damage our libido theory in the judgement of many readers. Schreber's 'rays of God', composed of a condensation of solar rays, nerve fibres and spermatozoa, are in fact nothing other than the libidinal investments, concretely represented and projected outwards, and so lend his delusion a striking conformity with our theory. The fact that the world has to end, because the patient's ego draws all the rays to itself, that later, during the process of reconstruction, he feels anxious concern that God might break his ray-connection with him, these and various other details of the formation of Schreber's delusion sound almost like endopsychic perceptions of the processes that I have assumed here to be constitutive for the understanding of paranoia. I am able, however, to call on a friend and expert in the field to bear witness that I developed the theory of paranoia before the contents of Schreber's book came to my notice. It will be for posterity to decide whether there is more delusion in the theory than I might like, or more truth in the delusion than others are today willing to believe.

Finally, I would not wish to finish this study, which in itself is merely a fragment of a greater, connected whole, without giving a preview of the two principal theses towards the verification of which the libido theory of the neuroses and psychoses is orientated: that the neuroses are essentially produced out of the conflict between the ego and the sexual drive and that their forms retain the imprints of the developmental history of the libido – and of the ego.

(1911 [1910])

Notes

1. Further confirmation can be found in the analysis of the paranoiac J. B. by A. Maeder ['Psychologische Untersuchungen an Dementia praecox-Kranken', *Jb. psychoanalyt. psychopath. Forsch.* 2] (1910). I regret that I have not been able to read this study at the time of writing my own.

2. I. Sadger ['Ein Fall von multipler Perversion mit hysterischen Absenzen', *Jb. psychoanalyt. psychopath. Forsch.* 2] (1910). Freud, *A Childhood Memory of Leonardo da Vinci's* (1910).

3. *Three Essays on the Theory of Sexuality* (1905).

4. Or in the *elementary language* as Schreber would say.

5. *Three Essays on the Theory of Sexuality* (1905). For the same view and formulation, cf. Abraham (loc. cit.) and Maeder (loc. cit.).

6. Jalāl al-Dīn Rūmī, as translated by Rückert; quoted from Kuhlenbeck's Introduction to Volume V of the works of Giordano Bruno.

7. A differently motivated type of 'end of the world' arises at the climax of love's ecstasy (cf. Wagner's *Tristan and Isolde*); here it is not the ego but the specific object that draws in all the investments given to the external world.

8. Cf. Abraham [op. cit.] (1908) and Jung [op. cit.] (1907). In Abraham's short work we find almost all the essential viewpoints of the present study of the case of Schreber.

9. Perhaps not only the libidinal investment but also any form of interest, including the investments that proceed from the ego. See the discussion of this question below.

10. Cf. [F.] Riklin ['Über Versetzungsbesserungen', *Psychiat.-neurol. Wschr.* 7] (1905).

Postscript

In the treatment of the case history of Justice Schreber I have intentionally restricted myself to a minimum of interpretation and can trust in the fact that any reader with psychoanalytic training will have derived more from the material communicated here than I have explicitly stated, and that he will not have found it difficult to draw the connecting threads more tightly together and to reach conclusions towards which I only gesture. A happy coincidence, which brought the Schreber autobiography to the attention of other authors included in the same volume as my paper, also gives some idea of how much is still to be gained from the symbolic content of the fantasies and delusional ideas of the paranoiac with such creative intelligence.[1]

Since the publication of my study of Schreber, a chance addition to the store of my knowledge has now put me in a position to give one of his delusional claims its more proper due and to recognize how rich are its *mythological* relations. On pp. 41–3 I mention the patient's special relationship to the sun, for which I duly gave the explanation of a sublimated 'father symbol'. The sun speaks to him in human words and so reveals itself to him as a living being. He has the habit of abusing it, shouting menacing words at it; he also declares that its rays pale before him when he is turned towards it and speaking loudly. After his 'recovery', he boasts that he can look calmly into the sun and is only very modestly dazzled by this, which was of course not possible before (note on p. 139 of Schreber's book).

The mythological interest is attached to this delusory prerogative of being able to look into the sun without being dazzled. In Reinach we read that the natural historians of antiquity deemed eagles alone to be capable of this,[2] who as inhabitants of the highest zones of the air became particularly intimately related to the heavens, to the sun, and to lightning.[3] The same sources also report, however, that the eagle subjects his young to a trial before recognizing them as legitimate. If they do not manage to look into the sun without blinking they are cast out of the nest.

There can be no doubt about the significance of this animal myth. What is ascribed to animals here is undoubtedly only what is a hallowed custom among humans. What the eagle undertakes with his young is an *ordeal*, a trial of origin, as these are reported among the most various peoples of ancient times. Thus the Celts who lived along the Rhine entrusted their newborn to the waters of the river in order to be convinced that they were really of their own blood. The tribe of Psylli from what is now Tripoli, who laid claim to being descended from snakes, subjected their children to contact with the same snakes; those of legitimate birth were either not bitten or were quick to recover from the effects of the bite.[4] The assumption underlying these trials takes us deep into the *totemic* thinking of primitive peoples. The totem – the animal or animistically conceived force of nature, from which the tribe traces its origin – spares the members of the tribe like its own children, just as they worship it and may come in turn to spare it as the father of their tribe. Here we find ourselves among matters that seem to me to be destined to enable a psychoanalytic understanding of the origins of religion.

The eagle that has his young look into the sun and requires that they should not be dazzled by its light is behaving, then, like a descendant of the sun, submitting his children to the ancestral trial. And when Schreber lays claim to being able to look into the sun unpunished and without being dazzled he has retrieved the mythological expression for his filial relationship to the sun and given renewed confirmation to our view of the sun as a symbol of the father. We should recall that Schreber freely gives vent to his family pride during his illness ('The Schrebers belong to the highest heavenly nobility'),[5] and that we found in his childlessness a human motive for his falling ill with a feminine wishful fantasy, so that the connection between his delusory prerogative and the foundations o͡f his illness appears clear enough to us.

This small Postscript to the analysis of a paranoiac may illustrate how well-founded is Jung's assertion that humanity's powers to form myths are not extinguished, but that they create today, in neuroses, the same psychic products as they did in the most ancient of times. I would like to take up once more a suggestion made previously by asserting that the same is true of the forces that create religions. And I believe that the time will soon come to extend a proposition, which we psychoanalysts voiced long ago, to add to its individual content, conceived of ontogenetically, an anthropological supplement, to be conceived of phylogenetically. What we said was: In dreams and in neurosis we find the *child* once more, with the peculiarities of its thinking and of its emotional life. To this we would add: and also the *savage*, the *primitive* human being, as he presents himself to us in the light of the study of antiquity and of other peoples.

(1912)

Notes

1. Cf. Jung ['Wandlungen und Symbole der Libido', Jb. psychoanalyt. psychopath. Forsch. 3 and 4] (1911, pp. 164 and 207); [S.] Spielrein [Über den psychologischen Inhalt eines Falles von Schizophrenie (Dementia praecox)', *Jb. psychoanalyt. psychopath. Forsch.* 3] (1911, p. 350).

2. [S.] Reinach [*Cultes, mythes et religions*] (1905–12), Vol. III (1908), p. 80. (After [O.] Keller [*Die Thiere des classischen Alterthums in culturges-chichtlicher Beziehung*], 1887).

3. Images of eagles were applied to the highest points of the temples to function as 'magical' lightning conductors (S. Reinach, loc. cit.).

4. See Reinach's references, loc. cit. and ibid., I, 74.

5. *Memoirs* (p. 24). 'Adel' [nobility] is related to 'Adler' [eagle].

Printed in the United States
by Baker & Taylor Publisher Services